Tristan und Isolde.
Luzern 1 Mai 59
Dritter Aufzug
Erste Scene
Mässig langsam
Vorhang auf.
Kurwenal an Tristans Lager
Hirt

CHARLES OSBORNE

WAGNER

and his world

with 142 illustrations

CHARLES SCRIBNER'S SONS
NEW YORK

1982

On the half-title page: The first page of
an orchestral sketch for the beginning of
the third act of *Tristan und Isolde*, begun
at Lucerne on 1 May 1859.

Frontispiece: Chalk drawing of Wagner
by Franz von Lenbach (*c.* 1874).

Printed in Great Britain
Library of Congress Catalog Card Number 76–56892

ISBN 0–684–14892–7

Watercolour, dating from 1840, of the street in Leipzig where Wagner was born. The house itself, 'The Red and White Lion', is on the left.

TWO GREAT COMPOSERS of opera were born in 1813: Giuseppe Verdi, in the Duchy of Parma, then part of Napoleon's empire but soon to become Austrian; and Richard Wagner, in Saxony, where Napoleon's troops were busy fighting the combined forces of Russia and Prussia. Both men were to become actively engaged in revolutionary movements; indeed politics would strongly influence their choice of operatic subject and even their music. Both were innovatory artists, geniuses who completely changed the face of opera both in and beyond their own countries: Verdi's achievement was to humanize Italian opera, to transform it from show business to art; Wagner's path lay in a different direction. By what might be thought of as a dehumanizing process, he led German opera back to the realm of myth and the old Northern gods. Opera, potentially the highest of the art forms, combining as it does elements of them all, was flexible enough to be extended in opposite directions by the genius of these two men.

5

Ludwig Geyer (above), Wagner's putative father, was an actor by profession, though he also studied law and art. For a time he earned his living as a portrait painter. This self-portrait dates from around 1806.
The oil portrait of Johanna Wagner (right), the composer's mother, was painted by Geyer in 1813, the year in which Wagner was born.

Yet in the second half of the twentieth century we look back to find that the practical Italian's influence has been more lasting on opera than that of the theoretical German. Wagner is credited with influence, of a baleful nature, not upon opera but upon political thought and action in Germany in the 1920s and 1930s. Not only are his theories on nationalism and race supposed to have contributed to the rise of Nazism, but his music, we are invited to believe, also played its part. Almost anyone capable of responding at all to Wagner's music will admit that it can somehow directly address itself to one's unconscious. So if the music of Verdi could be thought, as it certainly was in its own day, to have incited patriotic Italians to rise against their Austrian overlords, might not the potent spell of Wagner's music have had the power to affect the common unconsciousness of an entire nation?

Karl Friedrich Wagner was a local government official who worked with the Leipzig police force; his wife Johanna was the daughter of a miller. The Wagner family has been traced back in Saxony to the mid-seventeenth century, but it is most likely that Karl Friedrich was not the father of Richard, Johanna's ninth child, born on 22 May 1813. Six months later Karl Friedrich died of typhoid, but by this time his wife had already become intimate with an actor and painter, Ludwig Geyer, whom she married the following year. The strongest likelihood is that the father of the child baptized Wilhelm Richard Wagner in St Thomas's, Bach's old church, was Geyer.

Possibly of Jewish origin, he was connected both with the legal profession and the stage, and was himself something of a dilettante. As an actor he made a reasonable living, usually by playing villains; he also accepted commissions as a painter. He sang well enough to be engaged for operas, and also wrote plays. He was keen that Richard, legally his stepson, should become a painter and attempted to give him lessons, but these were discontinued when it became obvious that Richard had no talent for the visual arts.

Geyer was a member of the theatre company in Dresden, so the Wagner-Geyer family, which now included a tenth child, a daughter born six months after the wedding, took up residence in the Saxon capital. Richard was sent to school in the village of Possendorf, near Dresden, and was allowed to have piano lessons, even though his mother had informed the composer Weber, a friend of the family, that the lad had given no indication of possessing musical talent. When Geyer lay dying, the eight-year-old Richard, having been summoned home to the bedside, played a folksong on the piano which caused the dying man to remark: 'Perhaps he does have a talent for music.' Several of Richard's elder brothers and sisters were

Coloured lithograph of the churchyard of St Thomas's, Leipzig. On the right is the Thomaskirche where Wagner was baptized on 16 August 1813. The centre building is St Thomas's School, attended by the composer in 1830-1. To its left is the hall in which his C major symphony was played in 1832.

Cartoon of the composer Carl Maria von Weber conducting a rehearsal of his opera *Der Freischütz* at Covent Garden. Weber's music, and *Der Freischütz* in particular, strongly influenced Wagner.

soon to embark upon musical or theatrical careers, but his now twice-widowed mother probably hoped that her younger children would take up something other than the stage. After Geyer's death, Richard and his brother Julius went to live with Geyer's brother, Karl Friedrich Geyer, a goldsmith in Eisleben, where Julius was apprenticed to the goldsmith and Richard attended his second school. Returning home to Dresden a year later, he was enrolled at the Kreuz-schule as Wilhelm Richard Geyer, the name by which he continued to be known until his confirmation at the age of fourteen when he reverted to his legal name of Wagner.

Carl Maria von Weber was artistic director of the German Opera in Dresden, where he was a great popular hero. His opera, *Der Freischütz*, had been produced in Berlin with enormous success, and subsequently at virtually every other German opera-house, including Dresden, where young Richard Geyer was completely entranced by it. This, the music of German folksong, purified and somehow transmogrified for the stage, was the first music to speak directly to him, and his own operas were, in due course, to be founded upon it.

When Richard was thirteen, his sister Rosalie accepted a theatrical engagement in Prague and went to live there, accompanied by her mother and most of the family. Richard remained in Dresden and boarded with the parents of a schoolfriend, but was taken to Prague for a brief winter holiday. The next year he returned to Prague as part of a walking tour with his schoolfriend, Rudolf Böhme. The old baroque city and its associations enchanted him: so did the two attractive daughters of Count Pachta, with whom his sisters had become friendly. It was here, too, that he first got to know the works of E. T. A. Hoffman whose tales of the macabre made a great impression on him. He returned reluctantly to Dresden and to school.

Contemporary portrait of Rosalie Wagner, Richard's sister.

Wagner was never, academically, a good student, and his formal education was decidedly scrappy. Later he was to become busily autodidactic, but his knowledge of any one subject was never deep. Nor was he ever much of a linguist, barely managing to master German grammar, let alone the structure of a foreign language. The criticism usually made of Wagner's voluminous prose is that it is woolly minded, and that his thought was notoriously imprecise and confused. Yet it is possible that he thought clearly enough (there is nothing the matter with his musical thought), but that he was simply unskilled in the use of words. That he experienced the artist's urge to communicate was evident at quite an early stage and his first attempts at artistic expression were, in fact, literary ones. He wrote a number of poems while still at school, and convinced that for him literary distinction was just around the corner, he embarked upon the composition of a tragedy for the stage, *Leubald und Adelaide*. In his memoirs, *Mein Leben*, the mature composer recalls:

Unfortunately, the manuscript of this drama has been lost, but I can still see it clearly in my mind's eye. The handwriting was extremely affected, and the tall, backward-sloping letters with which I had hoped to give it a certain distinction reminded one of my teachers of Persian hieroglyphics. I had constructed my play largely upon Shakespeare's *Hamlet, King Lear* and *Macbeth*, and Goethe's *Götz von Berlichingen*. The plot was actually a modified version of *Hamlet*, the difference being that my hero was so completely overwhelmed by the ghost of his father, murdered in similar circumstances, that in his vengeance he resorts to dreadful deeds of violence. With the number of murders on his conscience piling up, he eventually takes leave of his senses.

When another sister, Luisa, accepted an engagement at the theatre in Leipzig, the family moved back there, and Richard was forced to change schools again. He enjoyed life in Leipzig, not so much for the activities at his school, the Nicolaischule, which he attended for two and a half years, but for the liveliness of the Leipzig University students, their clubs and societies, their conversations on literature, theatre, music, politics, philosophy, even their theatrical style of

Drawing made in 1832 of Adolf Wagner, brother of Wagner's legal father Carl Friedrich Wagner. Adolf was well known in Leipzig as a man of letters and it was to his 'Uncle Adolf' that the young Richard submitted his earliest literary efforts for judgment.

dress. Now in his mid-teens, he was eager to learn, from student acquaintances and from his Uncle Adolf, his father's brother, who enjoyed a local reputation as a man of letters. He even sent him *Leubald und Adelaide* to read, though his uncle was profoundly unimpressed by it. He frequented the theatre and the opera-house, and was never to forget a performance of Beethoven's *Fidelio* in which the role of the eponymous heroine was performed by the great Wilhelmine Schröder-Devrient, who only seven years earlier had sung the role in Vienna to the admiration of Beethoven himself. Young Richard was so moved by Schröder-Devrient that he rushed out of the theatre and wrote a note to her, 'declaring that from that moment my life had acquired its real meaning, and that if in the future she should ever hear my name praised she must remember that it was she who, on that evening, made me what I then swore I would become'. Schröder-Devrient must have been impressed by this impulsive fan letter, for she kept it, and years later when she met Wagner she was able to quote it from memory.

In his sixteenth year, the embryonic dramatist now turned his serious attention to the technique of musical composition. From a library he borrowed Johann Bernhard Logier's *Method of Thorough-Bass*, from a theatre violinist named Müller he took lessons in harmony, and from a study of Mozart's *Don Giovanni* and other works he learned

how to read a score. Within a few weeks he had begun to compose: a piano sonata, an aria, a pastoral play with music and a string quartet. Wagner was now preparing to enter the University of Leipzig, and first enrolled at the Thomasschule for several months. Here he helped to organize a student club and attended its initial meeting arrayed extravagantly in white leather breeches and jackboots. There was at this time a great deal of unrest in Leipzig, generated largely by the July Revolution in France; curiously, the Leipzig students appear to have been a predominantly conservative body, for they enthusiastically answered the call to help the police protect property from the mob.

Frustrated by general indifference to his earliest compositions, Richard for a time neglected music, throwing himself instead into student social life. He enrolled at the university as a music student, which entitled him to join the Saxonia Club in whose colours he delighted to parade. He drank heavily, took up gambling, and even began rashly to challenge to duels the university's more experienced swordsmen. He must, too, have been a boring and boorish companion at this time of his life, with his propensity to harangue his acquaintances in the thick Saxon accent he was to retain unadulterated to his death, and with his inability to tolerate any viewpoint but his own.

Eventually, of course, he emerged from this period of adolescent confusion and began to devote himself to the study of harmony and

The soprano Wilhelmine Schröder-Devrient (1804–60), whom Wagner greatly admired and for whom he wrote the roles of Adriano in *Rienzi*, Senta in *Der fliegende Holländer* and Venus in *Tannhäuser*. She was as much renowned for her dramatic genius as for her vocal abilities.

counterpoint with Christian Theodor Weinlig. After a year, at the end of which Weinlig used his influence to achieve publication of a piano sonata by his pupil, Richard went on to compose another piano piece which is of interest because it contains adumbrations of ideas that were to mature in the operas. He also composed two overtures which were played at Leipzig concerts, and several other songs, arias and choruses. With Count Vincnz Tyszkiewicz, a Polish revolutionary whom he had met in Leipzig, Richard visited Brünn (now Brno), the capital of Moravia, and then travelled on alone to that Mecca of all musicians, Vienna. There he was entranced by the gaiety and frivolity of the Viennese, by the waltzes of Strauss and Lanner, and by the magic plays with music, by Raimund and others, which were a unique Viennese genre, the genre from which Mozart's *Die Zauberflöte* (The Magic Flute) had sprung. The influence of these plays can be traced not only in Wagner's first opera, *Die Feen* (The Fairies), but throughout his entire *œuvre* up to his final work, *Parsifal*, whose magician Klingsor is an admittedly distant relative of the fairy-tale personages of the *Zauberpossen*, the magical plays of Vienna.

Wagner returned home via Prague, where a C major symphony he had composed was rehearsed by the orchestra of the Conservatorium, and subsequently given its first public performance with moderate success at one of the concerts of the famous Leipzig Gewandhaus Orchestra. Eager to begin work on an opera, he wrote a libretto, *Die Hochzeit* (The Wedding), and began to compose the music for it, but soon abandoned the work. In February 1833, now aged twenty, he secured a position at the theatre in Würzburg through the influence of his brother Albert, who was the company's leading tenor. Richard was happy to leave Saxony for neighbouring Bavaria, thus evading the military service he would shortly have been required to undertake. In Würzburg he worked as coach for the chorus and soloists, and began to learn the theatre's operatic repertory, which included such works as Meyerbeer's *Robert Le Diable*, Marschner's *Der Vampyr* and Bellini's *La straniera*. For the latter two operas he composed additional arias to suit the local singers, which was then a customary procedure.

It was during his year at Würzburg, one of practical operatic experience in the theatre, that Wagner wrote both the libretto and the music of *Die Feen*, his first complete opera. Taking his plot from *La donna serpente* by the eighteenth-century Venetian playwright Carlo Gozzi, Wagner altered and adapted freely, complicating an already complex fairy-tale, and overloading it with symbolism. Prince Arindal, while out hunting, encounters a beautiful and mysterious woman, Ada, with whom he falls in love. They marry,

Title page (right) of the manuscript of *Die Feen*, Wagner's first completed opera, composed between 20 February and 27 December 1833 (except for the overture, which he wrote in January of the following year) but not performed until 1888. The last scene of the opera (below) in a drawing by G. Franz from the Leipzig *Illustrirte Zeitung* of 28 December 1889.

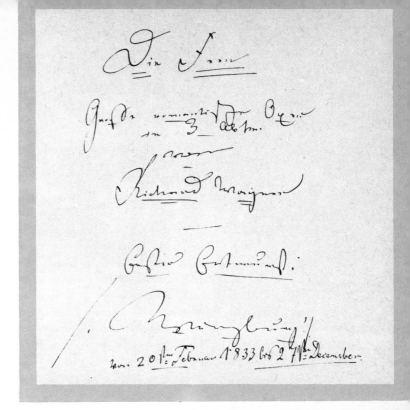

The composer Felix Mendelssohn-Bartholdy (1809–47). Apart from being jealous of Mendelssohn's youthful success, Wagner also resented that the composer never acknowledged receiving the symphony he had sent him and never alluded to it when they later met.

and Ada extracts a promise from Arindal that he will not attempt to discover anything about her. When, after eight years, he does ask the forbidden question, wife and castle suddenly disappear. Ada's problem is that she is half-fairy and half-mortal: it is only by subjecting both herself and her beloved to a series of cruel tests that she can become fully human. Not until Arindal has penetrated into the Underworld to rescue her are they reunited, and even then it is not by Ada becoming mortal but by Arindal being granted fairy status and immortality.

Thus, with his very first opera, Wagner plunged into that world of myth and fairy-tale which he was creatively to inhabit for the remainder of his life. Musically, however, *Die Feen* represents a false start, for Wagner not only chose the kind of subject which the more established German composers of his day tended to favour, but also imitated their style. This is not particularly surprising when one considers the composer's extreme youth: he was only twenty; but in view of the direction his mature genius was to take, and the grandiose scale of his later achievement, it is, perhaps, a trifle odd to find so little trace of originality or individuality in his first opera. Examining *Die Feen* now, with the benefit of hindsight, it is not difficult to discern adumbrations of musical and dramatic themes which were to be more fully worked out in the operas of Wagner's maturity. But to return to the comparison with his great Italian contemporary: while Verdi's first opera made it obvious that a new voice was being heard,

there was nothing in *Die Feen* to indicate to Wagner's fellow musicians that this was the work of a powerful and original talent. Much of the orchestral writing is pastiche Mendelssohn, while certain effects are borrowed from Weber and, in particular, Marschner, whose three operas, *Der Vampyr*, *Der Templer und die Jüdin* and *Hans Heiling*, had obviously deeply impressed the young Wagner.

Yet almost before he had completed *Die Feen*, which was never performed during his lifetime, Wagner's disillusionment with the prevailing style of German gothic-horror romanticism had begun. In the theatre at Würzburg he had been exposed to recent Italian operas and, though he affected to despise the simple orchestration of the Italians and their apparently easy access to melody, he could see that, aesthetically, their operatic style was obviously superior to the laboured pedantry of what was being composed in Germany. He returned to Leipzig early in 1834, and there in March he attended a performance of Bellini's *I Capuleti ed i Montecchi* in which his idol Schröder-Devrient sang the role of Romeo.

To see the daring romantic figure of the youthful lover against a background of such obviously shallow and empty music prompted one, at all events, to meditate doubtfully upon the cause of the great lack of effect in solid German music as it had been applied hitherto to the drama. Without for the moment plunging too deeply into this meditation, I allowed myself to be borne along with the current of my youthful feelings, then roused to ardour, and turned involuntarily to the task of working off all that brooding seriousness which in my earlier years had driven me to such pathetic mysticism.

Vincenzo Bellini (1801–35), the Italian composer whose operas Wagner conducted in Magdeburg and Riga. In 1837 Wagner wrote a brief article on Bellini and also conducted a performance of his opera *Norma*, into which he inserted a bass aria of his own composition.

Silhouette of Wagner, executed by an unknown artist in Magdeburg in 1835, while Wagner was engaged there as conductor.

The typically grudging tone of the admission that he had been moved by Bellini's art need not obscure the fact that Wagner, right at the outset of his career, found himself at a crossroads. That there was no future, artistic or professional, in continuing to produce imita~ tions of Marschner was clearly apparent. Marschner, as it turned out, was to prove perfectly capable of imitating himself. Though Wagner continued to hope for a production of *Die Feen*, which was being considered by the Leipzig Opera, he began to turn his thoughts towards the composition of an opera in the Italian manner. He and his friend Theodor Apel set out on a tour of Bohemia, during which Wagner began to sketch the rough draft of a new libretto. Perhaps Bellini's Romeo and Juliet opera had set him thinking of Shakespeare (though Shakespeare's play was not the main source of *I Capuleti ed i Montecchi*) for the play which he took as the starting~point for his libretto was *Measure for Measure*. Not too much creative work, however, was done during the Bohemian trip. In Prague, Wagner introduced his friend to the Pachta household and its nubile daughters, and was himself in lighthearted mood throughout the whole of his stay there. His escapades included climbing along the second~floor window~ledge of his hotel in his underwear, and leading a noisy rendition of the forbidden 'Marseillaise' in the middle of the night. It was as though he was celebrating his farewell to youth.

On the recommendation of the *Kapellmeister*, the chief conductor, at Leipzig, Wagner was now offered, and accepted, an engagement as conductor of the opera company at Magdeburg. During the summer months the company played at the spas of Rudolstadt and Lauch~ städt, and it was in Lauchstädt that Wagner joined the company, making his début conducting what must have been a quite dreadful performance of *Don Giovanni*, with poor singers and an inadequate orchestra which had never rehearsed the opera. But it was here that he met Minna Planer, the beautiful young leading lady of the theatre company, who was three years his senior. Before long, they had become lovers.

As he rapidly gained experience during the winter months in Magdeburg, Wagner began to acquire a local reputation as a con~ ductor. Unfortunately, he also acquired a reputation for extravagance, loose living and reluctance to pay his debts. Before long he was being pressed by a large number of tradesmen, to whom he referred contemptuously as a 'cursed rabble of Jews'. He had one hope of satisfying his creditors: with the proceeds of a concert he was allowed to give for his own benefit. He persuaded the famous Schröder~ Devrient to appear, but the concert turned out to be a fiasco. Refusing to believe that the distinguished singer was really likely to appear for the benefit of the disreputable Wagner, and suspecting that they

were the victims of a hoax, the citizens of Magdeburg stayed away *en masse*. Madame Schröder-Devrient sang to a meagre audience, and then took a seat in the stalls to listen to the remainder of the programme, conducted by Wagner. Unfortunately he had miscalculated the acoustics of the hall which proved so reverberant that the performance of Beethoven's 'Battle' Symphony, complete with cannon and musketry, threatened to deafen those few who had come to hear it. This was more than Schröder-Devrient could stand, Wagner wrote years later, 'even out of friendship for me. When, therefore, the English made a fresh, desperate assault upon the French position, she took to flight, almost wringing her hands. Her action became the signal for a panic-stricken stampede. Everyone rushed out; and Wellington's victory was finally celebrated in a confidential outburst between myself and the orchestra alone.'

Minna Planer, Wagner's first wife. When they first met, she was the leading lady of a provincial theatre company.

Wagner retreated to Leipzig with his brown poodle Rüpel, in order to escape his creditors, but returned to Magdeburg after a summer of unemployment and recommenced his relationship with Minna. He also completed work on his Shakespeare-based opera, *Das Liebesverbot* (The Ban on Love), and the impresario of the Magdeburg opera company agreed to produce it at the end of the season. Because of the expense involved in mounting the work, an arrangement was made whereby the management would take the entire proceeds of the first performance, the second performance constituting the composer's benefit. The company found themselves having to learn the opera in ten days, and circumstances were not improved by the fact that the composer acted as both conductor and stage director. On the first night, the tenor forgot much of his part, and resorted to pieces from *Fra Diavolo* and *Zampa*, operas by Auber and Hérold in which he felt more at home. On the second night, Wagner's benefit, the composer peered through the curtain to find an audience of three Jews: a Madame Gottschalk who had befriended him, her husband and 'a Polish Jew in full dress'. Suddenly there was a commotion backstage. The husband of the prima donna had attacked the young and handsome second tenor whom he suspected of being his wife's lover. With alacrity the entire company joined in the quarrel, and the second performance of *Das Liebesverbot* failed to take place.

In his very free adaptation of Shakespeare's *Measure for Measure*, Wagner transferred its action from Vienna to Sicily, and turned the play into a contrast between the puritan Teutonic spirit and the sensual warmth of the South, the composer's sympathies being decidedly with the childlike Mediterraneans. In the process, the play's ironies were flattened out into farce. Musically, the opera is shamelessly eclectic; the Marschner influence, though much weakened, is still apparent, but it is the music of Rossini, Donizetti and Bellini of which Wagner's fussily uninventive score is reminiscent. Listening to it today, one is struck by his first use of the theme, known as the 'Dresden Amen', which was to reappear later in *Tannhäuser* and, in a different form, in *Parsifal*. In *Das Liebesverbot* it is sung by an off-stage chorus of nuns to the words 'Salva regina coeli'.

Wagner's flirtation with Italian models resulted in an even less satisfactory work than his earlier attempt to imitate Weber and Marschner. Yet *Das Liebesverbot* has its interest: its libretto, though a travesty of Shakespeare's play and propagating ideas of dubious aesthetic or moral value, is really much better planned and shaped than those of his mature operas; for these he did not have the advantage of a play already in existence whose structure he could utilize. The slipshod dramatic form and frequently mediocre versifying of the

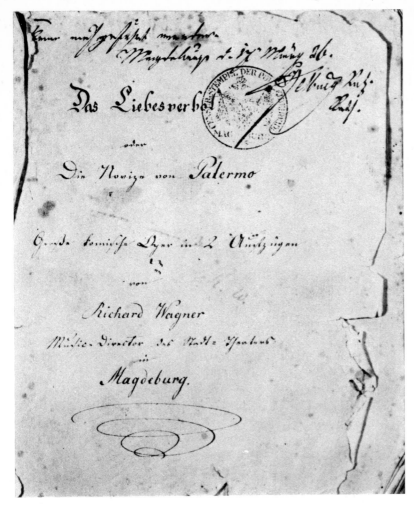

mature operas must, however, be given their due since they did help musical masterpieces into being. But the existence of *Das Liebesverbot* causes one to wonder whether Wagnerian masterpieces of an even higher quality, operas whose texts would have been the equal of their music, might have been composed had Wagner not deluded himself into the belief that he possessed literary talent. In later life he was to describe his second opera as 'atrocious, abominable, nauseating': this it certainly is not, though it contains few traces of Wagner's later genius.

In 1836 Wagner married Minna Planer, and she procured him an engagement in the theatre at Königsberg where she was employed for the forthcoming season. From the beginning, the marriage was anything but placid. After some months, Minna ran away to her parents' home in Dresden, unable to face Wagner's way of life

Title page of the text of Wagner's second opera, *Das Liebesverbot*, which he wrote while employed in Magdeburg. It carries a stamp of the censor's office in Magdeburg, dated 17 March 1836.

which entailed continual hiding from creditors. Wagner, thinking she had eloped with a Königsberg merchant named Dietrich whom he knew to be interested in her, immediately instituted divorce proceedings, but then as quickly withdrew them. Shortly afterwards Minna again disappeared, and this time there could be no doubt that Dietrich was involved. Wagner had by now been engaged by the opera-house in Riga, the Latvian (then Livonian) capital which, though governed by Russia, was at that time a prosperous Baltic outpost of German culture. While waiting to go to Riga, he spent several weeks with his sister Ottilie and her husband Hermann Brockhaus, an authority on Eastern languages. For some time, Wagner had been toying with the idea of breaking into French grand opera, and he now began to plan an opera to be based on the novel *Rienzi*, by the English writer Henry Bulwer-Lytton, which he had just read in a German translation.

When, in due course, Wagner arrived in Riga, he found that Minna was willing to return to him. Overcome with joy, he bought two black poodles. In October 1837, Minna and her sister Amalie, a mezzo-soprano, made the journey to Riga. For a time the family was relatively happy. Wagner, bored with the repertory he had to conduct, devoted much of his energies to the composition of *Rienzi*. But it was not long before the situation deteriorated. First the sisters began to quarrel, apparently because a young Russian officer fell in love with Amalie and married her a year later. During that time, the two sisters managed to live in the same house without addressing a single word to each other. Then the theatre manager, Holtei, while openly displaying his antipathy to Wagner, at the same time began to make unwelcome advances to Minna. Finally Wagner's old creditors from Magdeburg and Königsberg caught up with him and demanded justice under Russian law. In addition, he had contracted a number of fresh debts in Riga. At the instigation of his creditors, Wagner's passport was confiscated, and to make matters worse he learned that his contract at the theatre would not be renewed. Flight appeared to be the only way out of the Wagner family difficulties.

At this point, Abraham Möller, an old friend of Wagner's from Königsberg, came to his aid. Möller offered to convey Wagner and Minna in his carriage at top speed across the Russian frontier to an East Prussian port. The family pet was now a large Newfoundland dog called Robber, who also had to be squeezed into the carriage. Near the frontier, they were forced to wait until sundown, 'and had ample leisure in which to realize that we were in a smugglers' drinking den, which gradually became filled to suffocation with Polish Jews of most forbidding aspect'. During the night they ran across the

ditch which lay the entire length of the frontier, managing to avoid the Cossack guards. At the Prussian port of Pillau, where the coach overturned and deposited Wagner on a pile of manure, they boarded a small sailing vessel, the *Thetis*, whose captain agreed to take them to London without passports. The journey should have taken no more than eight days, given the good weather which was reasonably to be expected in summer. But it was three weeks before they reached London after a singularly adventurous and eventful voyage. Part of Wagner's account of the sea journey is worth quoting for the light it throws on one of his most popular operas:

Watercolour by Baron von Leyser of the finale of Act II of *Rienzi*. This is not the 1842 Dresden première but a performance the following year in which the part of Adriano, pictured kneeling, was taken by the contralto Henriette Kriete. Rienzi, on horseback, was sung by Joseph Tichatschek, who had also taken the role at the première.

There was an elderly and peculiarly taciturn sailor named Koske, whom we observed carefully because Robber, who was usually so friendly, had taken an irreconcilable dislike to him. Oddly enough, this fact was to add in some degree to our troubles in the hour of danger. After seven days sailing we were no further than Copenhagen where, without leaving the vessel, we seized an opportunity of making our very spare diet on board more bearable by various purchases of food and drink. In good spirits we sailed past the beautiful castle of Elsinore, the sight of which brought me into immediate touch with my youthful impressions of *Hamlet*. We were sailing all unsuspecting through the Cattegat to the Skagerack, when the wind, which had at first been merely unfavourable, and had forced us to a process of weary tacking, changed on the second day to a violent storm. For twenty-four hours we had to struggle against it under disadvantages which were quite new to us. In the captain's painfully narrow cabin, in which one of us was without a proper berth, we were a prey to sea-sickness and endless alarms. Unfortunately, the brandy cask, at which the crew fortified themselves during their strenuous work, was let into a hollow under the seat on which I lay at full length. Now it happened to be Koske who came most frequently in search of the refreshment which was such a nuisance to me, and this in spite of the fact that on each occasion he had to encounter Robber in mortal combat. The dog flew at him with renewed rage each time he came climbing down the narrow steps. I was thus compelled to make efforts which, in my state of complete exhaustion from sea-sickness, rendered my condition every time more critical. At last, on 27th July, the captain was compelled by the violence of the west wind to seek a harbour on the Norwegian coast. And how relieved I was to behold that far-reaching rocky coast, towards which we were being driven at such speed! A Norwegian pilot came to meet us in a small boat, and, with experienced hand, assumed control of the *Thetis*, whereupon in a very short time I was to have one of the most marvellous and most beautiful impressions of my life. What I had taken to be a continuous line of cliffs turned out on our approach to be a series of separate rocks projecting from the sea. Having sailed past them, we perceived that we were surrounded, not only in front and at the sides, but also at our back, by these reefs, which closed in behind us so near together that they seemed to form a single chain of rocks. At the same time the hurricane was so broken by the rocks in our rear that the further we sailed through this ever-changing labyrinth of projecting rocks, the calmer the sea became, until at last the vessel's progress was perfectly smooth and quiet as we entered one of those long sea-roads running through a giant ravine – for such the Norwegian fjords appeared to me. A feeling of indescribable content came over me when the enormous granite walls echoed the hail of the crew as they cast anchor and furled the sails. The sharp rhythm of this call clung to me like an omen of good cheer, and shaped itself presently into the theme of the seamen's song in my *Fliegender Holländer*.

The *Thetis* had to cope with an even worse storm and a narrow escape from shipwreck before it sighted the shores of England, but in mid-August the mouth of the Thames was eventually reached. When Richard, Minna and Robber arrived in London, they found lodgings in Old Compton Street in Soho.

London at the very beginning of Victoria's reign was a city that retained much of its Regency style and gaiety, and the Wagners enjoyed their few days there before making the Channel crossing to

Boulogne. On the steamer, Richard made the acquaintance of the Mansons, a Jewish mother and daughter who were friends of the celebrated composer Meyerbeer, at that time living in Boulogne. The Mansons gave Wagner a letter of introduction to Meyerbeer, who received the young composer graciously, allowed him to read aloud a large part of the libretto of *Rienzi* and agreed to examine the score. He also gave Wagner introductions to men of influence in the Parisian music world, including both the administrator and the conductor of the Paris Opéra. This was a gesture of generous disinterest, for Meyerbeer was the reigning idol of Parisian grand opera and might well not have wished to encourage possible younger rivals or successors. Again Wagner was indebted to a Jew, and in his memoirs years later he repaid the debt in characteristic fashion: 'The years had not yet given [Meyerbeer's] features the flabby look which sooner or later mars most Jewish faces, and the fine formation of his brow round about the eyes gave him an expression of countenance that inspired confidence.' In journalistic articles he wrote anonymously and scurrilously of Meyerbeer, referring to him on one occasion as a 'filou' or pickpocket.

Lithograph of Giacomo Meyerbeer (1791–1864), the most popular composer of French grand opera during Wagner's years in Paris. Wagner learned much from Meyerbeer's operas but bitterly attacked him in various articles, including 'Jewishness in Music'.

Richard, Minna and the giant Newfoundland, Robber, finally arrived in Paris where Richard began to make contacts with people of influence in musical and operatic circles. Money was scarce, and he began borrowing from Eduard Avenarius, who was shortly to marry Wagner's sister Cäcilie, and who found lodgings for the Wagners in Paris. Most of Richard's close friendships were with the German community, for his knowledge of the French language was virtually non-existent. He remained monolingual throughout his life. Though he met Heine, Berlioz and several other prominent artists, his attitude towards them was compounded too strongly of envy to allow him to benefit from their friendship or advice. After he had pawned Minna's jewellery, clothes and finally her wedding ring, and had then sold the pawn tickets, Wagner resorted to borrowing further from in-laws and acquaintances, and even to accepting gifts of money from friends of friends, including a wealthy Jewish merchant named Axenfeld. He was not in the habit of repaying any of these debts: in fact, he may have been the first artist to put into reasonably successful practice the theory that the world owed him a living.

Out of respect for Meyerbeer, Duponchel, director of the Opéra, agreed to see Wagner, though it was not to be expected that the Paris Opéra would rush to commission an opera from a young, completely unknown foreign composer. Yet, at Meyerbeer's urging, the Opéra's chief conductor, Habeneck, accepted Wagner's *Columbus* Overture for concert performance. Despite his lack of familiarity with the language, Wagner began to compose songs to French texts and attempted to sell them to French singers, without conspicuous success. He managed to get his opera *Das Liebesverbot* accepted by the Théâtre de la Renaissance, once again through Meyerbeer's influence, but the theatre went bankrupt before it could be produced, and Wagner decided that Meyerbeer was somehow to be held responsible. The new director of the Paris Opéra was prevailed upon to listen to parts of the opera played on the piano by its composer, an audition which was also attended by the famous librettist Scribe. But *Das Liebesverbot* made no effect, and Wagner began work on *Der fliegende Holländer* which he at first envisaged as a short one-act curtain-raiser.

The financial situation was now desperate, his brother-in-law was no longer prepared to support the Wagners and even Robber had run away to find a master better able to feed him. Months after he had disappeared, Wagner caught sight of Robber in the distance and called him. When the dog recognized his old master, he fled for the second time. The lowest point of the family misfortunes was reached in October 1840, when Wagner was imprisoned for debt. There he remained for several weeks until Minna's begging letters, drafted by

Wagner, to Theodor Apel, a Leipzig friend of his schooldays, bore fruit. After his release he attempted to earn a living making arrangements of operas and other music, and accepted journalistic assignments, most of which came his way through the good offices of the German-Jewish music publisher Moritz Schlesinger, who was a friend of Meyerbeer. But journalism paid little, and Wagner's German had to be translated for publication.

Though jealous of any composer achieving success in Paris, Wagner entertained a healthier respect for Berlioz than for his benefactor Meyerbeer. The two men met in Paris on several occasions. Berlioz praised some of Wagner's journalism, while Wagner, many years later in his memoirs *Mein Leben*, professed a guarded admiration for the French master: 'But while admiring this genius absolutely unique in his methods, I could never quite shake off a certain peculiar feeling of anxiety. His works left me with a sensation as of something strange, something with which I felt I should never be able to be

Portrait of the composer Hector Berlioz (1803–69) by Courbet. Wagner, though admiring several of Berlioz's works, disliked the text of *The Trojans*. Berlioz made the mistake of reading this to Wagner, who quite possibly saw it as a rival to his vast *Ring* project.

familiar, and I was often puzzled at the strange fact that, though ravished by his compositions, I was at the same time repelled and even wearied by them.' (Berlioz, in *his Memoirs*, referred to Wagner's 'intellectual laziness, against which he should be more on his guard'.) In truth, the artistic ideals of the two composers were fundamentally opposed. The classical discipline which lay securely at the heart of Berlioz's romanticism seemed bland and soulless to Wagner, while Berlioz must have thought Wagner's view of the roles of drama and music in opera completely wrong-headed.

In June of the following year, 1841, came the news that *Rienzi*, which Wagner had managed to complete, probably while he was in prison, and which he had sent to the Dresden Opera, had been accepted for performance; he had been recommended to the management by Meyerbeer. By this time, Wagner had exhausted every possibility of succeeding in Paris. Yet he remained there, or rather in Meudon, a village outside Paris, for most of the year to work on *Der fliegende Holländer*, which had grown beyond the proportions of a mere curtain-raiser. When the opera was completed, Wagner sent it to Berlin. He and Minna had by now returned to Paris, and once again their debts were paid by patient and generous friends. One or two more commissions came his way, including one from a Jewish composer, Josef Dessauer, who asked Wagner to provide a libretto for him, which the impecunious composer did for a fee of 200 francs. He also found time to draft the synopsis of a drama to be called *Die Sarazenin*, for possible future use as a libretto.

Rienzi had been accepted by Dresden, but had not yet been produced, and further delays were now imposed. Wagner began to realize that, if his opera was ever to be staged, it was necessary for him personally to agitate for its production. In March 1842 he learned that the Berlin Opera had accepted *Der fliegende Holländer*, on Meyerbeer's suggestion, to whom, therefore, Wagner was once again indebted. Obviously the time was ripe for his return to Germany. The necessary funds were borrowed, and Richard and Minna set off by coach to Dresden.

Among the pieces which Wagner wrote for various magazines in Paris are three short stories, 'Eine Pilgerfahrt zu Beethoven' (A Pilgrimage to Beethoven), 'Ein glücklicher Abend' (A Happy Evening) and 'Ein Ende in Paris' (An End in Paris), which were first published, in French translation, in the *Revue et Gazette Musicale de Paris* in 1840 and 1841. For these stories Wagner invented the character of an unknown, middle-aged German composer who worships Beethoven, and, in the first story, makes a pilgrimage from the north of Germany to Vienna to see the great man. In the second story, the unknown composer arrives in Paris where, after a year or two of vain attempts to make a career in music, he dies in extreme poverty, his final days being related in the last of the three stories. Though hardly great examples of the storyteller's art, all three are fascinating for the light they throw both on Wagner's thought processes and on his opinion of himself. The opening story is told in the first person by the impecunious middle-aged composer, but in the other two, set in Paris, the narrator has become a younger composer, doubtless Wagner himself, who attempts to befriend the hapless older man. At the same time, the older, disillusioned musician retains several of Wagner's own qualities as a composer. In addition, the first story contains a touching portrait of Beethoven, on whose personality Wagner would clearly like to have modelled himself, had not circumstances continually conspired against him:

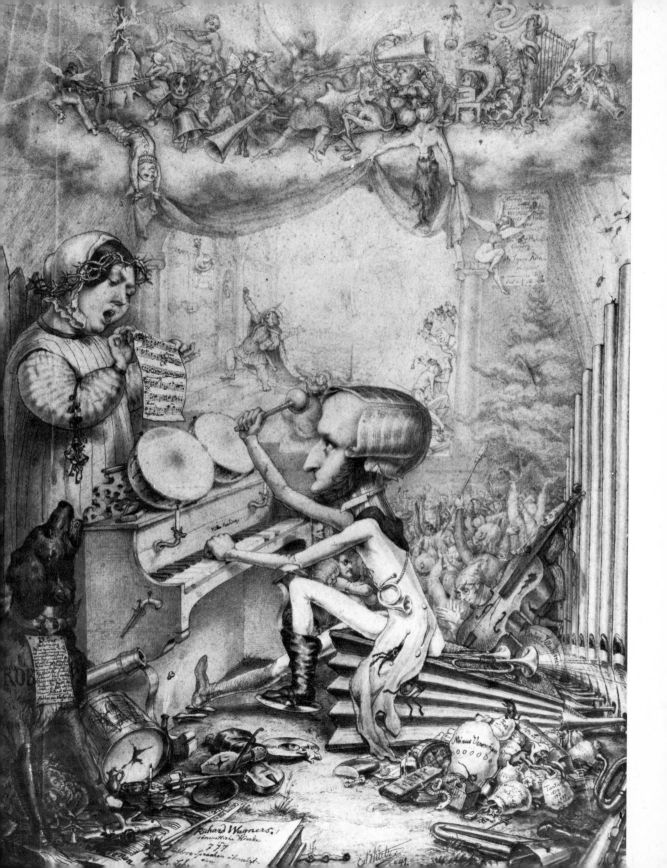

He was clad in somewhat untidy house-clothes, with a red woollen scarf wrapped round his waist. Long, bushy grey hair hung in disorder from his head, and his gloomy forbidding expression was far from reassuring. We took our seats at a table strewn with pens and paper. . . . At last he began, in grating tones: 'You come from Lembach?' I was about to reply, when he stopped me. Passing me a sheet of paper and a pencil, he added: 'Please write. I cannot hear.'

I knew of Beethoven's deafness, and had prepared myself for it. Nevertheless it was like a stab through my heart when I heard his hoarse and broken words, 'I cannot hear.' To stand joyless and poor in the world, to be uplifted by nothing but the power of music, and then to be forced to say, 'I cannot hear'! That moment gave me the key to Beethoven's exterior, the deep furrows on his cheeks, the sombre dejection of his look, the set defiance of his lips. He could not hear!

At the end of the final story, the honest, mediocre old German musician on his deathbed articulates his creed, which is obviously also that of the romantic young author of the story. The dying com-poser's opening words curiously anticipate those of the artist Louis Dubedat in Bernard Shaw's *The Doctor's Dilemma*:

'Now', the dying man continued, after a pause occasioned by his growing weakness, 'now one last word on my belief. I believe in God, Mozart and Beethoven, and likewise their apostles and disciples. I believe in the Holy Spirit and the truth of the one, indivisible Art. I believe that this Art proceeds from God, and lives within the hearts of all artists. I believe that he who once has bathed in the sublime delights of this high Art is consecrated to Her forever, and never can deny Her. I believe that through this Art all men are saved, and therefore each may die of hunger for Her. I believe that death will give me my highest happiness. I believe that on earth I was a jarring discord, which will at once be perfectly resolved by death. I believe in the last judgment, which will condemn to fearful pains all those who in this world have dared to play the huckster with chaste Art, have violated and dis-honoured Her through the evil of their hearts and the ribald lust of their senses. I believe that these will be condemned through all eternity to hear their own vile music. I believe, upon the other hand, that true disciples of high Art will be trans-figured in a heavenly veil of sun-drenched fragrance of sweet sound, and united for eternity with the divine fount of all Harmony. May mine be a sentence of grace! Amen!'

In April 1842 Richard, then aged twenty-nine, arrived in Dresden with his wife Minna. As soon as he had arranged accommodation for them both, Wagner went off to Leipzig to visit his mother whom he had not seen for six years. From Leipzig he made his way to Berlin to find out how plans for the projected production of *Der fliegende Holländer* were advancing. Here he found a deteriorating situation. The opera-house had a new *Intendant*, or artistic director, a man who had already rejected the opera for Munich; Wagner's champion, Meyerbeer, was on the point of leaving Berlin. By the end of April Wagner had returned to Dresden. During a hiking holiday in the Bohemian mountains at the beginning of the summer,

Caricature of Wagner by E. B. Kietz, Paris, 1840-1 (left). Many allusions are made here to the composer's life and work.

he began to sketch out the libretto for a new three-act opera which he thought of calling *Der Venusberg* but which in due course became *Tannhäuser*. In the middle of July, back in Dresden, Wagner began to involve himself actively in preparations for the forthcoming première of *Rienzi*. The opera cannot have been an easy one for the recently opened Dresden opera-house to stage: it was inordinately long, its large cast and choruses were expensive to dress, and the orchestra found the music extremely difficult. Fortunately the principal singers were first rate. Joseph Tichatschek was cast in the title-role, and the famous Wilhelmine Schröder-Devrient sang Adriano, despite the fact that she did not care for the role and that her figure was hardly seen to its best advantage in male costume. The first performance on 20 October began at six in the evening and ended shortly before midnight. On this occasion the stamina of performers and audience appears to have been greater than that of the composer:

I noticed that the first two acts had taken as long as, for instance, the whole of *Der Freischütz*. On account of its warlike calls to arms, the third act begins with an exceptional uproar, and when at its close the clock over the stage pointed to ten, which meant that the performance had already lasted a whole four hours, I became

Sketches of the cast for the première of *Rienzi*, from the Leipzig *Illustrirte Zeitung* of 12 August 1843. From left to right: Rienzi – Joseph Tichatschek (tenor); Irene – Henriette Wüst (soprano); Adriano – Wilhelmine Schröder-Devrient (mezzo-soprano); Colonna – Paul Dettmer (bass); Orsini – Michael Wächter (bass).

absolutely desperate. The fact that, after this act also, I was again loudly called for I regarded merely as a final courtesy on the part of the audience who no doubt wished to signify that they had had quite enough for one evening and would now leave the house in a body. As we still had two acts to go, I thought it certain that we should not be able to finish the piece, and considered apologizing for my lack of wisdom in not having previously effected the necessary curtailments. . . . But my astonishment at finding the audience still there in full muster, even in the last act towards midnight, filled me with unbounded perplexity. I could no longer trust my eyes or ears, and regarded the entire evening as a nightmare. It was past midnight, however, when for the last time I had to obey the thunderous calls of the audience, side by side with my faithful singers.

Rienzi, the earliest of Wagner's operas to have stayed, however precariously, alive, is the last in which any discernible trace of Parisian influence remains. It is cast in the five-act form of French grand opera, and its story of the struggle between the Orsinis and Colonnas in fourteenth-century Rome lends itself to spectacular stage treatment, ending as it does with the Capitol in flames, and the three principal characters perishing in the holocaust. There is much of Meyerbeer in the music, in the processional rhythms, the great choruses, even in the broad melody of Rienzi's prayer in Act V,

Lithograph, *c.* 1841, of the Dresden Court Theatre (left) and a view of the interior (below left). It was here that *Rienzi, Der fliegende Holländer* and *Tannhäuser* had their premières. Designed by Gottfried Semper and built between 1837 and 1841, the theatre was destroyed by fire in 1869 but was rebuilt to the same designs. It was again destroyed during the bombing of World War II.

Wilhelmine Schröder-Devrient (right), in a lithograph of 1840 by Hanfstaengl.

Rudolf Berger as Rienzi (right). Berger (1874–1925) began his career as a baritone and was much admired at Bayreuth as Amfortas, Gunther and Klingsor. After 1906 he became successful as a tenor in Berlin and Vienna, as well as at the Metropolitan Opera House, New York. Rienzi was one of his favourite tenor roles.

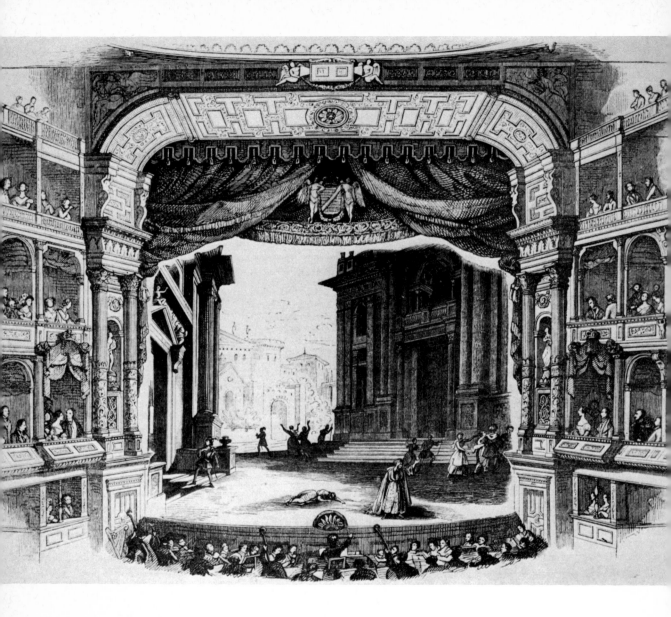

Illustration from the Leipzig *Illustrirte Zeitung* showing the final scene of Act IV of *Rienzi* at its première at the Dresden Opera on 20 October 1842.

though this particular theme, Janus-like, also faces towards the sweeping lines of mature Wagner. That *Rienzi* should still occasionally be performed, while *Die Feen* and *Das Liebesverbot* are almost totally neglected by professional opera companies, is somewhat unfair. The two earlier works are no less immediate in their impact than *Rienzi*, in which Wagner deliberately set out to compose an opera of the kind he thought Parisian audiences would appreciate, and succeeded all too well.

The first of Wagner's operas in which his genius shines forth unencumbered, unembarrassed by the past, is surely *Der fliegende Holländer*. Wagner first encountered the legend of the Dutchman in Heinrich Heine's *Memoirs of Herr von Schnabelewopski*, but the legend was not created by Heine and had been widely known for many years. A Dutch sea-captain swears that he will round a certain dangerous cape in rough weather, even if he should go on sailing until the day of judgment. As a result, he and his ship are thereafter condemned to sail on throughout eternity. In several accounts of the legend, the phantom ship hails passing vessels and asks them to deliver letters to relatives in Holland, letters which turn out to be addressed to people long since dead.

The story of the Dutchman is sometimes referred to as 'the English legend', and, although it may not have originated there, it certainly does make several appearances in English literature and drama in the early nineteenth century. An anonymous story, 'Vanderdecken's Message Home or The Tenacity of Natural Affection', appeared in *Blackwood's Magazine* in May 1821, and five years later a three-act play called *The Flying Dutchman or The Phantom Ship* was produced in London at the Adelphi Theatre. In 1839 Captain Marryat's novel *The Phantom Ship*, based on the legend, was published. Heine's picaresque novel mentions the Flying Dutchman in only one chapter, when the eponymous Schnabelewopski visits a theatre in Amsterdam and sees a play on the subject. The action of the play is described in detail by Heine, and includes an additional element lacking in earlier accounts of the legend: the possibility of the Dutchman's redemption through the love of a faithful woman. It was surely this which aroused Wagner's creative interest in the Dutchman, for the concept of redemption through love was thereafter to pervade almost every opera he wrote.

What was the precise meaning of the Flying Dutchman myth to Wagner? Fortunately he himself has revealed this in 'A Communication to my Friends':

The figure of the Flying Dutchman is a mythical creation of the folk: a primal trait of human nature speaks out from it with heart-enthralling force. This trait, in its most universal meaning, is the longing after rest from amid the storms of life. In the blithe world of Greece we meet with it in the wanderings of Ulysses and his longing for home, house, hearth and wife: the attainable, and at last attained, reward of the city-loving son of ancient Hellas. The Christian, without a home on earth, embodied this trait in the figure of the wandering Jew: for that wanderer, forever doomed to a long-since outlived life, without an aim, without a joy, there bloomed no earthly ransom; death was the sole remaining goal of all his strivings; his only hope, the laying down of being.

Portrait of Wagner by Jager.

It is curious that Wagner should have discovered elements of the Wandering Jew in the Dutchman myth; but in a sense it is understandable, for to him the Jew was someone greatly in need of a redemption which, in the Christian world, he could never find. Wagner's Dutchman, then, embodies the composer's earliest thoughts on the character and dilemma of the Wandering Jew, just as Kundry in *Parsifal* many years later represents his mature attitude to the subject. His Dutchman carries on his own shoulders the *Weltschmerz* of his race, and what he flees from is responsibility for the betrayal and murder of Jesus. Unlike the Wandering Jew, however, the Dutchman has the possibility of redemption in the faithful love of a woman. It is in contemplating this touch added by Heine to the legend that Wagner not only makes a creative leap into the world of the Goethean *Ewig-weibliche*, or eternal feminine, but also anticipates Ibsen in creating the new woman. The woman sought by Wagner's Dutchman is, as the composer himself points out, 'no longer the home-tending Penelope of Ulysses, as courted in the days of old, but the quintessence of womankind; and yet the still unmanifest, the longed-for, the dreamed-of, the infinitely womanly woman – let me out with it in one phrase: the woman of the future'.

Of course the Dutchman is not only the Wandering Jew. He is also, and most importantly, the artist, and not just the artist in general but Wagner in particular: Wagner, at this stage of his life, willing to accept Minna as his redeemer. In his first sketch for the opera, the heroine's name is not Senta but that of his own wife, Minna. Much of Wagner's own self-pity finds its way into the mouth of the Dutchman. Heine's cynical conclusion, that the moral of the play is that women should never marry Flying Dutchmen, and that men can expect no better from women than to go down and perish with them, is not one which Wagner would have had the humour to endorse. It is, in fact, Wagner's lack of humour, his ability to accept every aspect of the myth with the greatest seriousness, that enabled him to compose so hypnotically compelling an opera on the subject.

By the time, many years later, he came to see himself as Parsifal, Tristan and even, not so many years later, as Lohengrin, a certain garrulity and lack of proportion had begun to obtrude themselves upon Wagner's artistic instincts. In his twenties, when he wrote *Der fliegende ·Holländer*, composing the music in seven weeks, he was young enough for this not to be the case. *Der fliegende Holländer* is, indeed, Wagner's most concise work for the stage. Its libretto was initially planned in one long act, and Wagner's intention was always that it should be played straight through without breaks in the music. Practical considerations dictated the three-act structure at the opera's first performance, in Dresden in 1843 (the Berlin Opera having willingly, even enthusiastically, relinquished their rights to Dresden), but the opera has been produced in this century in its one-act version (for the first time in 1901 at Bayreuth). It gains immeasurably from being performed as Wagner originally intended it should be, with the postlude of one act flowing easily into the prelude of the next.

Poster for the Dresden première of *Der fliegende Holländer*, which took place on 2 January 1843.

Drawings from the Leipzig *Illustrirte Zeitung* of 7 October 1843. The three figures from *Der fliegende Holländer* (above) are the Dutchman, Senta and Erik, as portrayed by the artists of the Dresden première, Michael Wächter, Wilhelmine Schröder-Devrient and Herr Reinhold. In the final scene of the opera (below), Senta throws herself into the sea to prove to the Dutchman that she has not betrayed him, while the Dutchman's ship founders in the harbour.

The Steersman's Song from Act I of *Der fliegende Holländer* (right), reproduced in the Leipzig *Illustrirte Zeitung* of 15 July 1843.

Matrosenlied

Lied der norwegischen Matrosen.

Aus dem fliegenden Holländer von Richard Wagner.

Lebhaft, doch nicht zu schnell.

Gesang.

Piano.

Steuermann, laß die Wacht! Steuermann, her zu uns! He! He!

Je! Ha! Hißt die Segel auf! Anker fest! Steuermann her!

Fürchten weder Wind noch bösen Strand, wollen heute 'mal recht lustig sein! Jeder hat sein Mädel auf dem Land,

herrlichen Tabak und guten Brantewein! Huf saffa he! Klipp' und Sturm draus — Hallo he he!

Wagner's involvement in, and his intensification and humanization of, the Dutchman myth did not end with his composition of the words and music of the opera. He has left detailed and fascinating notes on how the characters are to be conceived and performed by the singers. An essay exists in which he goes, move by move, through the Dutchman's first scene, instructing the singer how and where to move, and on which bar to make what gesture; for example: 'With the ninth and tenth bars, during the solo from the drum, the Dutchman again advances two steps nearer to Senta.' Wagner is most interesting, in more general terms, on the character of Senta. She, after all, is his own invention, non-existent in the popular myth, and barely adumbrated in Heine, and he is concerned to ensure that she is not weakened by being portrayed sentimentally:

The role of Senta will be hard to misread; one warning alone have I to give: let not the dreamy side of her nature be conceived in the sense of a modern, sickly sentimentality! Senta, on the contrary, is an altogether robust Northern maid, and even in her apparent sentimentality she is thoroughly naïve. Only in the heart of an entirely naïve girl, surrounded by the idiosyncrasies of Northern nature, could impressions such as those of the ballad of the Flying Dutchman and the picture of the pallid seamen call forth so wondrous strong a bent as the impulse to redeem the doomed. With her, this takes the outward form of an active monomania such, indeed, as can be found only in quite naïve natures.

Der fliegende Holländer is Wagner's first real encounter with folk myth. But he came to it fully fledged, and the fruit of the encounter is an opera which is in no sense an apprentice work. That he was to deal differently with a different kind of myth in his masterpieces *Tristan und Isolde*, *Parsifal* and *The Ring*, does not invalidate the fresher, crisper, more Italianate approach of *Der fliegende Holländer*, a work so filled with strong passions that it has simply no time for weak longueurs.

The première of *Der fliegende Holländer* took place at the Dresden Opera on 2 January 1843, with Michael Wächter as the Dutchman and Wilhelmine Schröder-Devrient as Senta. Despite what Wagner referred to as the 'magnificent performance of my great artist', the occasion was not a blazing success, and not more than four performances were given. The composer blamed Wächter for this:

Unfortunately even Schröder-Devrient only saw when the rehearsals were too far advanced how utterly incapable Wächter was of realizing the horror and supreme suffering of my Mariner. His distressing corpulence, his broad fat face, the extra-ordinary movements of his arms and legs, which he managed to make look like mere stumps, drove my passionate Senta to despair. At one rehearsal, when in the great scene in Act II she comes to him in the guise of a guardian angel to bring the message of salvation, she broke off to whisper despairingly in my ear, 'How can I say it when I look into those beady eyes? Good God, Wagner, what a muddle you have made!'

The Dutch baritone Cornelius
Bronsgeest (1878–1957) in the title-
role of *Der fliegende Holländer* (below).
Bronsgeest had a distinguished
international career, but was
especially popular in Berlin where
he sang the Dutchman as well as a
number of Italian roles.

The famous Czech soprano Emmy
Destinn (1878–1930) as Senta in
Der fliegende Holländer (above). She
was much admired in this role when
she sang it for the first time at the
Bayreuth Festival in 1901.

Der Venusberg

romantische Oper in 3 Acten.

Personen.

Hermann, Landgraf von Thüringen.

Tannhäuser
Wolfram von Eschinbach
Walther von der Vogelweide
Biterolf
Heinrich der Schreiber
Reinmar von Zweter
} Ritter und Sänger.

von Ofterdingen + der Tugendhafte

Elisabeth, Nichte des Landgrafen.

Venus.

(: Thüringen :)

Act I

(: Im Venusberg. Tiefe Grotte durch rosiges Licht erleuchtet; bis in den fernsten Hintergrund sich ziehende Paare, in üppig-nachlässigen Stellungen; Nymphen in anmuthig wechselnden, verlockenden Stellungen u. Tänzen; Bacchantinnen, mit wilden Lustgebärden durchziehen in brausendem Tanze die Gruppen. — Im Vordergrund zur Seite erhöht Venus auf einem üppigen Lager ausgestreckt; Tannhäuser neben ihr knieend, das Haupt in ihrem Schoße. — In den tanzenden Gruppen tritt allmälig eine wollüstige Erschlaffung ein; rosige Wolken ... die Gruppen, wie ein anmuthiger Vorhang; ein schwüler Duft durchzieht die Grotte u. verhüllt nach u. nach die Gruppen gänzlich vor den Blicken des Zuschauers. — Bloß Venus u. Tannhäuser bleiben sichtbar. :)

(: aus dem fernen Hintergrund ein zartes Nachhallen des Gesanges der Sirenen: —)

Tannhäuser zuckt wie aus einem Traume auf, — Venus zieht ihn schmeichelnd zurück; er fährt mit der Hand über die Augen, als wolle er einen Traum festhalten. — Ven: „Wo bist du, Geliebter?" Tannh: „Zu viel! Zu viel! O, daß ich erwachte!" — Ven: „Sag, was dich kümmert!" — Tannh: „Ich träumte: mir war als hörte ich, was ich so lange vermißte — als hörte ich der Glocken frohes Geläute. — Sag mir, wie lange hört' ich's nicht mehr?" — Ven: „Was wandelt dich an? wohin verlierst du dich wieder?"

[illegible]

[illegible]

Morlacchi, the *Hofkapellmeister* or chief conductor to the court at Dresden, had died in the autumn of 1842. Early the following year the lifelong position was offered to Wagner who accepted with alacrity. He also persevered with the composition of *Tannhäuser* and had finished it by the spring of 1845. In the autumn the opera was produced in Dresden with Joseph Tichatschek in the title-role, Wagner's niece Johanna Wagner as Elisabeth and Schröder-Devrient as Venus. Though its initial reception was lukewarm, the opera caught on at its third performance. But four years were to elapse before it was staged elsewhere, and ten years or more before it was seen on important stages such as Berlin, Munich and Vienna. Wagner's essay on sacred and profane love was in general thought to be too slow and stately for its subject matter. Today the sojourn of Tannhäuser, the medieval knight, with Venus, the goddess of love, seems impossibly tame, while his spiritual relationship with the pure Elisabeth is singularly unconvincing. Certain set-pieces and arias, for instance Elisabeth's 'Dich, teure Halle' and Wolfram's 'O du, mein holder Abendstern', were appreciated by Wagner's early audiences, rather than the opera as a whole, and it is these arias which keep *Tannhäuser* alive today, though it has never attained the popularity of the earlier *Fliegender Holländer* or the later operas.

At the première of *Tannhäuser* in Dresden on 19 October 1845, the tenor Joseph Tichatschek (1807–86) sang the title-role (above left), while the composer's niece, Johanna Wagner (above), took the part of Elisabeth.

The first page of Wagner's initial prose sketch for *Tannhäuser* (far left). The original title, 'Der Venusberg', can be seen at the top of the page.

Even before the première of *Tannhäuser*, Wagner had begun to sketch the libretto of his next opera, *Lohengrin*, during a summer visit to the famous spa resort of Marienbad (now Mariánské Lázné) in Bohemia. He had taken with him a copy of the anonymous epic *Lohengrin*, which took such a hold of him as soon as he began to read it that he found himself excitedly drafting a libretto on the subject. This detailed preliminary prose synopsis, which was not published in full until 1936 in the Bayreuth Festival guide, differs in occasional details from the final libretto in verse. The differences, however, are not fundamental: they came about as Wagner the practical stage director prepared for public performance the work of Wagner the visionary poet-musician. The third Wagner, that less than completely trustworthy autobiographer, tells us that, when he read the libretto to friends in Dresden, Schumann failed to understand the musical form implicit in it, since there appeared to be no provision for individual musical numbers. 'I then had some fun in reading different parts to him in the form of arias and cavatinas, after which he laughingly declared himself satisfied.'

Costume designs by Flinzer (above) for the Dresden première of *Tannhäuser*. The characters depicted are, from left to right, Tannhäuser, Elisabeth, the Landgrave and Wolfram.

The second act of *Tannhäuser* (left) as staged at the Dresden première, depicted in a watercolour after Wilhelm Heine.

The music of *Lohengrin* was written during the next three years: a hasty outline sketch of the entire score, followed by detailed composition of the three acts, beginning with the third. By March 1848 the opera was complete; but by the time of its first performance under Liszt on 28 August 1850 in Weimar, Wagner had fled to Switzerland as a political refugee from Saxony. It was not until 1861 that he himself witnessed a performance of the work. The Weimar première, given with a company of inadequate singers and a far too small orchestra, obviously did considerably less than justice to *Lohengrin*, which was at first considered a failure. Nevertheless, the opera was staged throughout Germany during the following decade, and was eventually hailed as the apotheosis of the German romantic opera. By then, its composer had left German romantic opera behind him and was immersed in the creation of his new type of music-drama.

Lohengrin, in fact, stands at the crossroads. Romantic in its almost Pre-Raphaelite purity and its static, two-dimensional characterization, it also contrives to anticipate the direction Wagner was to take in his next work, *Tristan und Isolde*, by virtue of its delicate balance, though not yet complete fusion, of music and drama. The music was already being made subservient to the drama whenever Wagner felt a tension of interests. An important instance of this can be found in his letter to Liszt of 2 July 1850, only a few weeks before the opera's première:

Give my opera as it is, without cuts. Just one cut I myself prescribe: I want you to take out the second part of Lohengrin's Narration in the big final scene of the third act. After Lohengrin's words, 'Sein Ritter ich, bin Lohengrin genannt', fifty-six bars are to be omitted, down to 'Wo ihr mit Gott mich alle Landen saht'. I have many times performed the entire work to myself, and I am now convinced that this second section of the Narration can have only a chilling effect. The passage must also be omitted from the libretto.

The passage was dutifully removed by Liszt and has only rarely been heard since. Those who have heard a set of American gramophone records of the opera with the cut passage restored will know that, at this stage of his career, Wagner's artistic judgment was sound, and that *Lohengrin* is better without those fifty-six bars. It was later that a certain elephantiasis of the imagination set in.

Lohengrin was Wagner's sixth opera. It will be recalled that the elements of the supernatural and of redemption through love, which were now to remain constant preoccupations throughout his life, had already been present in his very first opera, *Die Feen*, and had reappeared in more mature form in both *Der fliegende Holländer* and *Tannhäuser*. With the exception of that magnificent hymn to national pride and artistic compromise, *Die Meistersinger von Nürnberg*, which

Portrait of Franz Liszt (1811–86) by Miklós Barabás, 1847 (left). Wagner was eventually to marry Liszt's illegitimate daughter Cosima.

Sketches by Wagner of stage designs for the first production of *Lohengrin* in Weimar (below).

Poster announcing the première of *Lohengrin* (left) at the Court Theatre, Weimar, on 28 August 1850. The opera was preceded by a prologue, honouring the memory of Goethe, written by Franz Dingelstedt and spoken by Herr Jaffé.

was still some years in the future, they were to be, in one form or another, the subjects of every opera and music-drama Wagner composed. The themes were interconnected: love triumphed over evil, but spiritual love triumphed over temporal, earthly passions. The conflict between the two worlds, the worlds of the flesh and the spirit, was Wagner's basic subject.

The word 'spiritual' has a meaning for some people, but not for others. Like so many problems, this can be reduced to one of semantics. We can substitute 'unconscious' or, if psychological terms are unacceptable, 'aesthetic'. For Wagner himself the terms were interchangeable. In 'A Communication to my Friends', he wrote: 'Elsa is the unconscious, the unvolitional, into which Lohengrin's conscious, volitional being yearns to be redeemed; but that yearning is itself the unconscious, unvolitional in Lohengrin, through which he feels himself akin in being to Elsa.' Elsewhere Wagner sees Lohengrin as saint and redeemer. But the most useful key to the understanding of who and what Lohengrin is, is the suggestion that he represents Wagner the misunderstood genius, just as Vanderdecken, the Flying Dutchman, represented Wagner the betrayed idealist, and Wotan was to represent Wagner the unheeded prophet. The tension between inner and outer world, sacred and profane, eternal and temporal, is also that which existed between Wagner the artist and his audience. It is upon this fact that, to a large extent, the shaky philosophical structure of Wagner's music-dramas is constructed. Inevitably, Wagner was led for a time seriously to contemplate Jesus as an operatic subject: Wagner as crucified Messiah. He actually sketched out a libretto, called 'Jesus of Nazareth'.

It is not to be thought that this self-identification with his heroes was necessarily a conscious act on Wagner's part. Writing to a friend in 1856, he says that the period in which he worked in response to his intuitions began with *Der fliegende Holländer*, and asserts that if in *Tannhäuser* or *Lohengrin* there is any underlying poetic theme, it must be looked for in the supreme tragedy of renunciation, the abnegation of the will, 'which is shown there as necessary and unavoidable, and alone capable of achieving redemption'. One does not have to read very far between the lines of this Schopenhauerian language to realize that Wagner is talking about art as much as philosophy. The plot of his *Lohengrin* plays fairer with his public than he himself does. By asking the forbidden questions, 'Who are you? Where do you come from?', Elsa does indeed lose her saviour Lohengrin, but with those same questions she regains her brother who is finally more real to her than the magical knight Lohengrin, because his only existence is in the real world. The visible world has its legitimate delights, and Wagner is not, after all, the only artistic

Prelude to Lohengrin, an oil painting by Fantin-Latour of 1902. The painting shows the descent of the Holy Grail to Titurel, an event which in fact does not occur in the opera but is depicted, according to Wagner himself, in the Prelude: 'Oh, that moment when the Grail appears before our eyes; what revelation of infinite splendour, what amazement in the soul; Art sanctified, the visible presence of God as beauty.'

genius. This is what, despite its author, the libretto of *Lohengrin* appears at this point to be saying. The libretto, however, is not simply a peg for the music to hang on. Despite the fact that its philosophical meaning and validity are open to question, it works magnificently in purely dramatic terms. Upon a two-dimensional, medieval fear of the unknown world, Wagner has superimposed a drama which is modern in its psychology and unerring in its poetic instinct. Thus he retains the best not of two apparent worlds but of three: the spiritual, the psychological and the aesthetic. It is the interplay between these three views of the world, in Wagner's music and his words, which makes *Lohengrin* a great opera.

Costume design for *Lohengrin* (above) by Julius Schnorr von Carolsfeld, 1860. Von Carolsfeld's son Ludwig was Wagner's first Tristan.

Title page of the libretto of *Lohengrin* (above right), published at the time of the Weimar première in 1850.

Lohengrin is the first opera in which Wagner makes complex use of the *leitmotif*, or guiding theme, a device on which he was increasingly to rely in his later works where characterization (as, for example, in *The Ring*) is virtually based on the *leitmotif* concept. Wagner did not himself invent the device, which is to be found in opera and instrumental music in the eighteenth century, as well as in more than one early opera by Verdi, but he did make much more exhaustive use of it than any other composer, so much so that the term has come now to be associated almost exclusively with him. In his first operas, *Die Feen*, *Das Liebesverbot* and *Rienzi*, the *leitmotifs* are crudely employed: themes associated with particular characters or situations are made to recur at appropriate moments. It is not until *Lohengrin* that Wagner makes more sophisticated use of the *leitmotif*, remodelling, reshaping and developing themes, and altering their orchestration to suit a changing dramatic situation, or to create a subtle nuance of expression. By the time he came to compose *The Ring*, his use of the device had become masterly in its complexity and in its uncanny power to affect the listener subconsciously.

The years 1848 and 1849 were critical for Wagner. At the beginning of 1848 his mother died; some weeks later revolution broke out in Paris and, almost simultaneously, in Vienna and Berlin. Wagner, involving himself in the revolutionary movement in Dresden, publicly proposed the freedom of the theatre from the control of the court and propounded a national union of composers and dramatists. In addition, he advocated generally curtailing the powers of the nobility and setting up a Saxon republic. The following year Wagner published a provocative essay, 'The Revolution', in the *Volksblätter*. He associated intimately with the Russian nihilist Bakunin and was very practically involved with the revolutionary group, even signing an order for a supply of hand-grenades. It is small wonder that eventually a warrant was issued for his arrest. In his autobiography, Wagner was to claim that he had been unjustly persecuted, that he had attended revolutionary meetings simply out of curiosity, as one might attend a play. In a sense it *was* a play, but Wagner was one of the actors, not a member of the audience. Even had he not been in danger of arrest, he would probably have had to flee from Dresden, for his debts were mounting and his creditors mobilizing. When the Dresden uprising failed, he and Minna, plus dog and cockatoo, managed to get out of the city, thus avoiding the Master's arrest for treason, a charge punishable by death.

Lithograph showing the Dresden Opera and the Zwingerstrasse in flames during the May uprising of 1849.

Richard Wagner
ehemal. Kapellmeister und politischer Flüchtling aus Dresden.

Die Nr. 140 der „Leipziger Zeitung" vom 20. Mai 1849 brachte folgenden Original-

Steckbrief.

Der unten etwas näher bezeichnete Königl. Kapellmeister

Richard Wagner von hier ist wegen wesentlicher Theilnahme an der in hiesiger Stadt stattgefundenen aufrührerischen Bewegung zur Untersuchung zu ziehen, zur Zeit aber nicht zu erlangen gewesen. Es werden daher alle Polizeibehörden auf denselben aufmerksam gemacht und ersucht, Wagnern im Betretungsfalle zu verhaften und davon uns schleunigst Nachricht zu ertheilen.

Dresden, den 16. Mai 1849.
Die Stadt-Polizei-Deputation.
von Oppell.

Wagner ist 37—38 Jahre alt, mittler Statur, hat braunes Haar und trägt eine Brille.

Warrant for Wagner's arrest, issued after the attempted revolution in Dresden in which it was assumed Wagner had been involved. The caption under the drawing reads, 'Richard Wagner, former *Kapellmeister* and political fugitive from Dresden', and the text of the warrant itself is as follows: 'The royal *Kapellmeister* described below, Richard Wagner of this city, has been summoned to appear before the authorities for taking part in riots which have occurred in this city, but has not as yet been found. All police officers are informed of the facts, and are ordered to arrest Wagner as soon as they find him, and to report the matter to us immediately.'

Mein Leben explains how Wagner made great efforts to rejoin his comrades on the barricades. The truth is that he got away as quickly as he could. With the help of his brother-in-law Wolfram, he reached Weimar, only to find that Liszt, who had invited him there to attend the production of *Tannhäuser*, was distinctly unenthusiastic about having a political refugee on his hands. Then Minna, having temporarily returned to Dresden, wrote to inform Wagner that the police had already been to their apartment. It was imperative that Wagner leave immediately, for no doubt the Weimar authorities would soon be asked to extradite him. Minna met up with him at the village of Magdala, but could not bring herself to accompany him into exile and, perhaps, years of penury and hardship. She returned to Dresden, while Wagner, armed with funds from Liszt and a false passport, made his way via Lindau and the Bodensee to Zürich and thence to Paris. Minna, meanwhile, seriously contemplated a permanent separation from her unsatisfactory husband. Yet when he left Paris after a few weeks and returned to Zürich, she joined him there and once more they set up house together. Wagner occupied himself with the production of articles on art and revolution, on German myth and on his concept of the art of the future; but these were restless days. He travelled to Paris and Bordeaux in fruitless attempts to advance his career or at least to raise money, and in the meantime had an affair with an English woman whose French husband had offered him an annual allowance. By July 1850 he was back again in Switzerland with Minna.

On 28 August 1850 Liszt's production of *Lohengrin* had its première at Weimar and eventually the news of its success reached Wagner. Other German opera-houses now began to interest themselves in his operas; suddenly he was accepted as the most outstanding German composer of opera of his day. Exiled in Switzerland, Wagner made plans for the future. For some years, he had had in mind an opera based on the old Norse myths, and he now set to work on a libretto entitled 'Siegfrieds Tod' (The Death of Siegfried), which was later to become *Götterdämmerung*, the last of the four *Ring* operas. At the same time, he contributed articles and essays to musical journals in which he attempted to clarify his thoughts on music and drama.

Wagner always considered himself to be both theorist and artist, yet for the most part his theories were somewhat absurd. It was fortunate that he possessed his genius for composition which ensured that, as a composer, he was not at the mercy of his own theories: although a simplification, it would be by no means an untruth to say that his masterpieces exist despite these theories, rather than because of them. In the majority of his essays it has to be admitted that both

Wagner's prose and his thought processes are extremely impenetrable, but the essays remain fascinating for the light they shed on the composer. It is also unfortunately true that some of Wagner's theories, which he was venal enough to adopt and discard always at the expedient moment, are as conscienceless as his character: a character which, as we have seen, allowed him to be callous in personal relationships, dishonest in business dealings and unreliable in most other matters.

Most of what Wagner had to say about music and drama can be found in four essays written between 1849 and 1851: 'Art and Revolution', 'The Art-Work of the Future', 'Jewishness in Music' and 'Opera and Drama'. His famous theory of the music-drama of the future in fact boils down to no more than an exhortation to the

Title page of Wagner's pamphlet 'Art and Revolution', published in Leipzig in 1849, in which Wagner discusses Greek drama and claims that only revolution can bring about the rebirth in Germany of such a communal, all-embracing art.

mid-nineteenth century to take opera as seriously as Handel, Gluck and Mozart had done. It is a pity that Wagner's vanity stood in the way of his heeding his own advice in this instance, for, instead of collaborating with a dramatist of distinction, he continued to write his own libretti. The results, especially in the later operas, are frequently as clumsily illiterate as the work of the Italian hack librettists whom he derides, and are additionally burdened by his Teutonic inability to be concise. The drama in the great operas of Wagner's maturity is provided entirely by the music, which is in places seriously hampered by the portentous doggerel churned out by the composer-as-poet. That much of it is of psychoanalytical interest has tended to obscure the fact that the libretto of, for instance, *Parsifal* is atrocious dramatic verse. The sad truth is that Wagner lacked any feeling for words as the raw material of art, though he certainly possessed the artist's instinct as far as his own requirements were concerned. Wagner the composer needed Wagner the poet: he would not have been happy with Goethe or Schiller.

The splendid pragmatic inconsistency of Wagner's temperament contributed more to his genius than did his theories. The revolutionary who was also a monarchist, the creator of the new who sought his inspiration in the old, the idealist who lived his own life disreputably: these were more closely employed in the creation of *Tristan und Isolde* and *The Ring* than the autodidactic theorist. By the time he had begun to draft the libretto of 'Siegfrieds Tod', Wagner had realized that his mission to revitalize the German theatre was to be a lifelong task, that it was to lead him back beyond the beginnings of German opera in the seventeenth century, beyond the sprawling drama of the Elizabethans, to the principles of classical Greek theatre. In 'Art and Revolution', the most important and certainly the most interesting of the four essays written at this time, his discussion of the theatre of ancient Greece leads him to the conclusion that, although its mechanics could hardly be made relevant to nineteenth-century Germany, its spirit could, and must, be revived. In the fusion of all the arts, of poetry, dance, drama, music and painting, into one all-embracing communal aesthetic experience lay the unique strength of Greek drama. Henceforth Wagner made it his mission to unite the arts again, after two thousand years, in a *Gesamtkunstwerk*, a complete work of art. From this intention, *The Ring* was eventually to emerge.

Wagner the polemicist published his notorious anti-Semitic tract, 'Jewishness in Music', under the inappropriate pseudonym of 'K. Freigedank' (K. Freethought), but was forced to acknowledge authorship when the literary (*sic*) style was immediately recognized as his. A brief quotation will suffice to reveal the intellectual level of this scurrilous piece of irrational abuse which ends by advocating the complete elimination of the Jews from German society and culture:

We are repelled in particular by the purely aural aspect of Jewish speech. Contact with our culture has not, even after two thousand years, weaned the Jew away from the peculiarities of Semitic pronunciation. The shrill, sibilant buzzing of his voice falls strangely and unpleasantly on our ears. His misuse of words whose exact shade of meaning escapes him, and his mistakenly placed phrases combine to turn his utterance into an unbearably muddled nonsense. Consequently, when we listen to Jewish speech we are involuntarily struck by its offensive manner, and thus diverted from understanding of its matter. This is of exceptional importance in explaining the effects of modern Jewish music on us. When we listen to a Jew talking, we are unconsciously upset by the complete lack of purely human expression in his speech. The cold indifference of its peculiar 'blabber' can never rise to the excitement of real passion. And if we, in conversation with a Jew, should find our own words becoming heated, he will always be evasive, because he is incapable of really deep feeling.

The essay is easily dismissed as the ravings of a mind distorted by hate and envy of such successful Jewish composers as Meyerbeer and Mendelssohn, but it should not be forgotten that, less than a century later, Germany was swayed by similar sentiments, similarly expressed, and advocating the same solution to the Jewish problem as that proposed by Wagner. The final sentence of his essay apostrophizes the Jewish race in these words: 'Remember that your redemption from the curse laid on you can be achieved by only one thing, and that is the redemption of Ahasuerus – decline and fall.'

Since one occasionally encounters the incredible assertion that Wagner was not anti-Semitic, it is interesting to note that in 1921 his son Siegfried, in a letter to a Bayreuth supporter who had apparently objected to the Festival's engagement of Jewish musicians, found it necessary to repudiate his father's attitude:

You suggest that we should turn all these people from our doors? Repulse them for no other reason than that they are Jews? Is that human? Is it Christian? Is it German? No! If we Germans wanted to behave like that, we would first have to become quite a different kind of people, with consciences clear as a mountain stream. . . . If the Jews are willing to help us, that is doubly meritorious, because my father in his writings attacked and offended them. They therefore have every reason to hate Bayreuth. Yet, despite my father's attacks, a great many of them genuinely admire his art. You must be well acquainted with the names of former Jewish supporters. Who, at that time, carried on a press campaign in support of my father? George Davidsohn and Dohm! You must also have heard of Tausig and Heinrich Porges. Josef Rubinstein arranged *Parsifal* for the piano, and Levi conducted the first performance. Even if, among a hundred thousand Jews, there were only one who was completely devoted to my father's art, I should feel ashamed to turn him away simply because he was a Jew.

Pastel of Mathilde Wesendonk and her son Guido by E. B. Kietz, Paris, December 1856 (above). Wagner was captivated by Mathilde, wife of Otto Wesendonk, and was inspired by her to compose *Tristan und Isolde*.

Wagner in 1859 (above right). This was said to be Mathilde Wesendonk's favourite likeness of Wagner.

Wagner's apotheosis of his anti-Semitism into aesthetic terms in *Parsifal* was still a long way off. For the present, he continued to work on the Siegfried myth. Realizing that 'Siegfrieds Tod' needed a preface, he drafted 'Der junge Siegfried' (The Young Siegfried). Under the title of *Siegfried*, it later fell into place as the third opera in the *Ring* cycle. This in turn led him back still further to *Die Walküre* (second in the cycle) and then *Das Rheingold* (the first *Ring* opera). By the end of 1852 the entire libretto of the four operas comprising the cycle *Der Ring des Nibelungen* was complete. Wagner had recently met in Zürich a rich silk merchant, Otto Wesendonk, whose young wife Mathilde had fallen completely under the Wagner spell. During the next few years, as Wagner was composing the music for his *Ring* operas, his friendship with Mathilde Wesendonk became more intimate. Wesendonk installed the Wagners in a house close to his own in Zürich, and it was here that Wagner turned aside from *The Ring* and, spurred on by his passion for Mathilde, began to compose his great romantic opera, *Tristan und Isolde*. The personal relationship of the Wagners and the Wesendonks soon became intolerable. The two women quarrelled openly, and when Minna intercepted a note which Richard had sent to Mathilde with a sketch of the Prelude

Watercolour dating from 1857 showing Zürich and its lake, with the Wesendonk villa on the hill at the left (above).

Wagner's house near the Wesendonk villa (left). This pencil drawing by G. Meyer, though dated 1851, was probably done c. 1857.

57

Otto Wesendonk, Wagner's benefactor, *c.* 1860.

to *Tristan*, a series of unpleasant scenes ensued. Wagner's behaviour to his benefactor was hardly calculated to improve matters: he even began to object to Wesendonk's presence in his own drawing-room when he and Mathilde were communing artistically. They had become collaborators, for Mathilde had written five poems under the influence of Wagner's *Tristan* libretto, and he in turn had set the poems to music, incorporating motifs from *Tristan*.

The Wesendonk Lieder do not constitute a song cycle and can be performed separately, though they relate closely to each other and to the emotional world of *Tristan und Isolde*. The third and fifth songs, 'Im Treibhaus' (In the hothouse) and 'Träume' (Dreams), were described by the composer as studies for the opera. 'Im Treibhaus' quotes from the Prelude to Act III, while 'Träume' is thematically related to the love music of Act II. Wagner wrote the songs for female voice and piano, but later orchestrated 'Träume' as a birthday present for Mathilde Wesendonk. The songs are frequently performed in orchestral versions made more than twenty years later by the Austrian conductor and composer Felix Mottl.

The foursome broke up when Minna was sent to Dresden to intercede for a pardon for Richard, and Otto Wesendonk took Mathilde on a visit to Italy. Before she left, Minna wrote to Mathilde: 'I must tell you with a bleeding heart that you have succeeded in separating my husband from me after nearly twenty-two years of marriage. May this noble deed contribute to your peace of mind, and to your happiness.' The unhappy Wagner, deprived of his benefactor, his muse-mistress and his domestic helpmate all at once, gloomily made his way alone to Venice to work on *Tristan und Isolde*. He was short of money, had recourse to pawnbrokers and wrote desperately to Liszt that 'Wagner does not give a curse for any of you, or your theatres or even his own operas. He needs money, that is all.' He also wrote to the Saxon minister of justice for permission to return to Saxony. The reply was discouraging, Saxony put pressure on Austria to expel him and in due course he was requested by the authorities to leave Venice, then under Austrian control.

During his seven months stay in Venice, Wagner had managed to complete the second act of *Tristan und Isolde*. The third act he finished in Lucerne, his place of retreat after his enforced departure from Italy. The Wesendonks had by this time returned to Zürich, and when Wagner paid them a visit he apparently found that Otto was prepared not only to resume relations with him, but even to help him again financially. Wagner felt it necessary that he should settle in Paris where he would be in close proximity to the major musical organizations, and Wesendonk agreed to purchase from him the copyrights in *Das Rheingold* and *Die Walküre* for the sum of 12,000

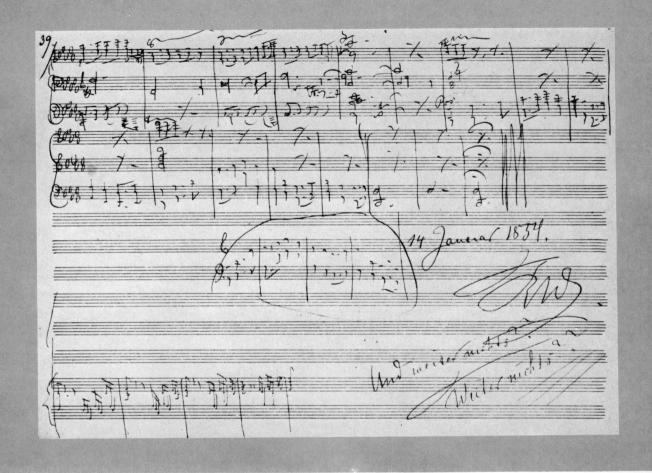

francs, the amount Wagner required to set himself up in Paris. He also required the presence of Minna, and wrote to her in Dresden where she was now in the care of a physician who was treating her for a heart condition and for general nervous exhaustion. Wagner urged her physician to make it clear to Minna that her health would never allow her to sleep with her husband again: it was not as a wife that he needed her, but as a housekeeper. In November 1859 Minna, dog and parrot arrived in Paris and the Wagners set up house yet again.

Wagner, having taken a three-year lease of a villa near the Champs Elysées, had spent much of the money he had received from Wesendonk in improving and decorating it. Now he set about promoting himself in Paris as a composer. His first steps were to hire a theatre in which to give concerts of his music and to attempt to persuade the Paris Opéra to produce *Tannhäuser*. In due course, the concerts were presented and the opera staged, though hardly to Wagner's advantage.

The closing bars of the compositional sketch for *Das Rheingold*, completed by Wagner on 14 January 1854. Under his initials are the words, 'Und weiter nichts? Weiter nichts??' (Nothing more? Nothing more??). The orchestration of the work was to occupy him until the following May.

Title page of a composition, 'Tannhäuser Quadrille und Walzer' (right), by the Viennese theatre composer and conductor Carl Binder, music director of the Carl Theatre, an operetta theatre in Vienna. The piece parodies Wagner, adapting themes from *Tannhäuser* to the rhythms of the quadrille and the waltz.

Minna, Wagner's first wife, in a watercolour by Clementine, Zürich, 1853. There was almost invariably a dog in the Wagner household.

The Parisian press was almost totally opposed to him, reviews of the concerts were uniformly hostile and attendances poor. The Paris Opéra appeared to be using delaying tactics, and it was only when Princess Metternich, the wife of the Austrian ambassador, used her influence to persuade the Empress to command a performance that *Tannhäuser* was finally presented.

Wagner had altered the opening scene of the opera, developing and expanding the ballet music. That he should have done this especially for Paris was not only desirable but obligatory, since all operas produced at the Opéra had to contain ballets. Yet there was still a problem: in *Tannhäuser* the ballet music occurred in the first act, but the dictators of Parisian taste were quite specific in their requirement that the ballet should be in Act II. This was an unwritten rule enforced by the fashionable young men of the Jockey Club, an

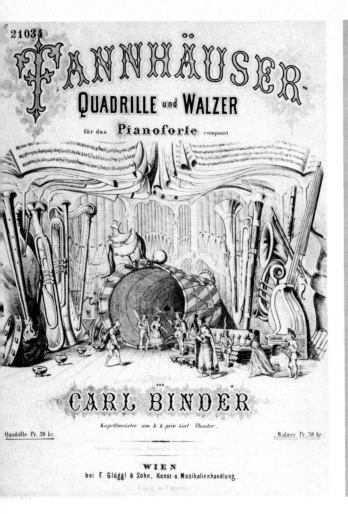

immensely conservative and philistine organization: its members liked to turn up at the Opéra just in time to see the ballet, or at any rate to appreciate the charms of the female performers and, besides, had to be given time to finish dining at a properly elegant late hour before strolling to the theatre. So M. Royer, the manager of the Opéra, attempted to impress upon Wagner the necessity of providing a ballet in Act II. He explained, as did several of the composer's friends, that it would be folly to incur the displeasure of the Jockey Club by failing to cater for its tastes. Wagner, however, was adamant that his *Tannhäuser* required no ballet in its second act. He hoped instead to please the Parisians with the rewritten and expanded sequence in Act I; if that was too early for the Jockey Club he was willing to stage a separate ballet at the end of the evening, after the opera.

Title page of Baudelaire's essay, 'Richard Wagner and *Tannhäuser* in Paris' (above), published in Paris in 1861. The essay was inspired partly by the scandals surrounding the first Paris production the same year.

Design by Philippe Chaperon for the third scene of Act II of *Tannhäuser*, as produced at the Paris Opéra in 1861.

Dismissing this problem from his mind, Wagner turned his attention to two new tasks: the supervision of a French translation of his libretto, and the selection of a suitable cast of singers. The principals eventually chosen were Albert Niemann, a *Heldentenor*, or heroic tenor, from Hanover, as Tannhäuser; Fortunata Tedesco, a voluptuously Junoesque soprano, as Venus; the twenty-one-year-old Marie Sax as Elisabeth; and an Italian baritone, Morelli, as Wolfram. Rehearsals commenced; there were 163 before the first night, most of them conducted by Wagner himself. The conductor of the actual performances, a mediocre musician named Dietsch, took over only at the final rehearsals. In due course, after a number of delays, arguments about the ballet and difficulties with the singers, dates were announced for the public performances, and a satisfactory dress rehearsal was held.

On the first night, 13 March 1861, despite the presence of the Emperor and Empress and the leaders of Parisian society, the performance was disrupted by organized demonstrations by the members of the Jockey Club, furious that the composer had disregarded their wishes concerning the ballet. At the second performance, five nights later, they continued their attack. Wagner recalls the incident in *Mein Leben*:

The first act promised well. The Overture was loudly applauded without a note of opposition. Madame Tedesco, who had been completely won over to her role of Venus by a wig powdered with gold dust, called out triumphantly to me in the manager's box that everything was now all right. But when shrill whistling was suddenly heard in the second act, Royer the manager turned to me with an air of complete resignation and said, 'Ce sont les Jockeys; nous sommes perdus.' From that time he gave up all attempt to resist them.

The impression made by this scene had a disastrous effect upon my friends. After the performance, von Bülow burst into sobs as he embraced Minna, my wife, who had not been spared the insults of those next to her when they recognized her as the wife of the composer. Our trusty servant Therese, a Swabian girl, had been sneered at by a crazy hooligan, but when she realized that he understood German, she succeeded in quietening him for a time by calling him 'Schweinhund' at the top of her voice.

The management was foolhardy enough to persevere with a third performance, at which the uproar continued:

The baritone Morelli found himself strangely perplexed when he had to weather the onslaught of these hooligans. I had explained to him in the minutest detail how to act his part from the time when Elisabeth disappears in the third act, until the beginning of his song to the evening star. He was not to move an inch from his rocky ledge, and from this position, half turning to the audience, he was to address his farewell to the departing lady. It had been a difficult task for him to obey my instructions, as he maintained it was against all operatic custom for the singer not to address such an important passage straight to the public from the footlights. When, in the course of the performance, he seized his harp to begin the song, there was a cry from the audience, 'Ah, il prend encore sa harpe!', upon which there was a universal outburst of laughter, followed by fresh whistling, so prolonged that at last Morelli decided boldly to lay aside his harp and step forward to the proscenium in his usual way. Here he resolutely sang his song to the evening star. Peace was, for a time, restored, and at last the public listened breathlessly to the song, showering the singer with applause at its close.

Isolated moments of the performance were heard in silence, but there were interruptions in every scene of the opera. Twice the performance was held up by fights in the auditorium lasting for a quarter of an hour or more. The greater part of the audience no doubt wanted genuinely to give *Tannhäuser* a fair hearing but, as Wagner himself realized, they were at a disadvantage. When all of his supporters were utterly exhausted with applauding and calling for order, and it looked as if the performance might be resumed, the Jockey Club began again

Tannhäuser and Venus, a gouache by
Eugène Delacroix.

cheerfully playing the whistles and pipes they had brought into the
theatre. The philistines triumphed, and *Tannhäuser* was not heard
again in Paris for thirty-four years. Princess Metternich, herself subjected to insults and ridicule at the first two performances, was heard
to say to one of her French friends: 'I've had enough of your free
France. In Vienna, where at least there is a genuine aristocracy, it
would be unthinkable for a Prince Liechtenstein or Schwarzenberg
to scream from his box for a ballet in *Fidelio*.'

Wagner, having been granted permission to return to any part of
Germany except Saxony, was now able to travel to various places
where production of his operas was under consideration. While
Minna returned to Dresden, he went to Weimar to visit Liszt, to
Vienna where he attempted to have *Tristan und Isolde* produced, to
the Wesendonks in Venice, where he decided to begin work on *Die*

Costume designs by Alfred Albert
for the Paris production of
Tannhäuser: above, Venus and
Tannhäuser, and below, Elisabeth
and a member of the chorus.

Meistersinger, and to Biebrich, near Mainz, which became his temporary headquarters. Here Minna arrived in a state of mental and physical near-collapse, demanding that he return to Dresden with her. Though Wagner visited her for four days in Dresden some months later, he and Minna had come to the parting of the ways. Realizing that their life together was an impossibility, he attempted to ensure that she would be provided for, and never saw her again. By the time she died, in January 1866, Wagner had become emotionally involved with Cosima von Bülow, illegitimate daughter of Liszt and the wife of the conductor Hans von Bülow, a Wagner disciple and friend, and ardent apologist for the Master's music and theories. Wagner had spent three years leading the nomadic life of a travelling musician, giving concerts of his own and other composers' works in Prague, St Petersburg, Moscow and Berlin, and during that time had lived briefly with other mistresses before he and Cosima, as he expressed it, 'sealed our vow to belong to each other alone'.

Now, however, another person forced an entry into Wagner's emotional life: none other than the eighteen-year-old Ludwig II, king of Bavaria, whose secretary brought to Wagner the curious news that king Ludwig was passionately interested in Wagner and his music, and wished to constitute himself the composer's protector.

Franz Liszt with his daughter Cosima (above left). Cosima married the German pianist and conductor Hans von Bülow (above) but left him for Wagner. During his years in Munich, von Bülow (1830–94) was one of Wagner's chief supporters.

Ludwig II's infatuation with Wagner was responsible for Wagnerian motifs creeping into the decoration of his royal castles. The two murals by Joseph Aigner shown here were executed for the castle at Neuschwanstein in 1881. One depicts Tannhäuser in the Venusberg with the goddess of love (far left, above), while the other shows Tannhäuser participating in the song contest (far left, below).

Painting by F. Dürck of Ludwig II
of Bavaria, 1864, the unstable young
monarch who loved Wagner and
his music (right).

Lithograph of Schloss Berg on Lake
Starnberg near Munich (below).
During the summer of 1864,
Wagner lived in a house
overlooking the lake, which had
been placed at his disposal by
Ludwig to facilitate their daily
meetings at the castle.

Wagner immediately went to Munich and became the close friend of the young homosexual king who was already well advanced towards the insanity in which he was to end his days. Wagner's entourage, consisting of Bülow and Cosima, turned the usual Wagner triangle into a rectangle. Cosima gave birth to Wagner's child, which Bülow accepted as his own, while Wagner received Ludwig's bounty and also his devotion, expressed by Ludwig in highly romantic terms:

The mean cares of everyday life I will banish from you forever. I will procure for you the peace you have longed for in order that you may be free to spread the mighty wings of your genius in the pure ether of rapturous art. O how I have looked forward to the time when I could do this! I hardly dared indulge myself in the hope of so quickly being able to prove my love to you.

Wagner soon persuaded the young king to agree to build him a theatre of his own. To Ludwig, who was to scatter fairy-tale castles round his kingdom, a mere theatre presented no great difficulty, and the architect Semper was summoned to prepare plans. But trouble was brewing for Wagner, for his relationship with the young king was considered scandalous by the Bavarian court. The old king, Ludwig I, had been thought disreputable because he had a mistress,

Cartoon, published in Munich, showing Wagner and Cosima walking along the Maximilianstrasse after a rehearsal of *Tristan und Isolde*, with Cosima's husband Hans von Bülow walking behind dropping pages of the score. 'Markes Klage', or king Mark's lament on finding that Isolde and Tristan are lovers, parallels Bülow's situation.

Arthur Schopenhauer (1788–1860), the German philosopher and author of *The World as Will and Idea* (above). Wagner's own theories were influenced by Schopenhauer's writings to which he was introduced in the early 1850s.

Lola Montez, and now the nickname of 'Lolotte' was conferred upon Wagner, who began to acquire the reputation of being an active homosexual. Ludwig had given Wagner an opulent apartment and the composer summoned Bertha, his Viennese milliner, to Munich to transform it into what a Wagner biographer has called 'a whorish fantasy of silks, satins, velvets and laces'. Ludwig's ministers, unable to take any more, began to plot Wagner's downfall. On the day *Tristan und Isolde* was to have had its première in Munich, Wagner received both the news that Minna lay fatally ill and a love-letter from Ludwig, who seemed to have cast himself as Isolde to Wagner's Tristan. In addition, Malvina Schnorr, who was to sing Isolde, had a sudden attack of catarrh and lost her voice. To cap it all, police officers entered Wagner's apartment with a warrant to attach his possessions for debt. Cosima was hastily dispatched to the royal treasury and returned with 2,400 florins. The première of *Tristan* was postponed, and the opera finally reached the stage on 10 June 1865. Many of Wagner's former friends and admirers were not present at this first performance, preferring not to expose themselves to the monster of vanity he had become. Of those who did witness the première of one of the great masterpieces of romanticism, few recognized its value, except perhaps the half-mad Ludwig who immediately announced it to be his favourite opera.

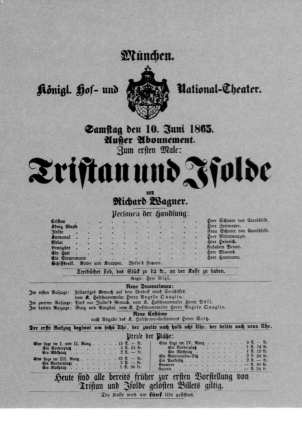

Tristan und Isolde, clearly, was written out of Wagner's love for Mathilde Wesendonk. It was also written under the influence of the philosopher Schopenhauer whose principal work, *Die Welt als Wille und Vorstellung* (The World as Will and Idea), Wagner had read in 1854. From Schopenhauer's belief that, in the world, there is so great a gap between the ideal and the real that suffering is a natural condition of mankind, grew Wagner's theoretical interest in renunciation of the worldly. But he, the most worldly of men, could embrace this belief only by turning from the outside world to the world of feeling, by renouncing day and its falseness and turning to night and love. The juxtaposition of hated day and longed-for night, the idea of day as mundane life and night as death-in-love, which permeates his libretto for *Tristan und Isolde*, is a specifically Wagnerian element, playing no part in the old Celtic myth or in the *Tristan* epic written by Gottfried von Strassburg in the thirteenth century.

Curiously, Wagner's original intention had been to write *Tristan und Isolde* in the style of Italian opera, as he expected this would earn the most money. He even began negotiations to provide such an opera for performance in Rio de Janeiro. It was only after his meeting with Mathilde Wesendonk in 1857 that the opera began to take shape in his mind in the form in which it was finally to emerge. When he

Playbill for the première of *Tristan und Isolde* at the Imperial Court and National Theatre, Munich, on 10 June 1865 (above left).

Ludwig Schnorr von Carolsfeld and his wife Malvina Schnorr von Carolsfeld as Tristan and Isolde in the first performance of the opera in Munich in 1865 (above).

The Royal Palace and, on the right, the Court Theatre, Munich (far left). In front of the palace is a monument to Max Joseph I. *Tristan und Isolde* had its première in this theatre in 1865, as did the first two *Ring* operas, *Das Rheingold* and *Die Walküre*, in 1869 and 1870.

Costume designs by Franz Seitz for the première of *Tristan und Isolde*. The characters depicted are, above, Tristan and Isolde, and below, Melot and Brangaene.

began to compose the music, all thoughts of deliberately copying the style of contemporary Italian opera were forgotten. The music, coming from deep within him, addresses itself to deep responses in its hearers, to the intuition, to the subconscious. It is music which is as susceptible to analysis as that of the composer's earlier operas, but to analyse *Tristan und Isolde*'s leading themes, its harmonies, its chromaticism, is more than usually irrelevant to an appreciation of the work itself.

Nevertheless, though one may be reluctant to theorize about *Tristan und Isolde*, it is in this opera that Wagner's theories of drama find their most felicitous expression. In *Tannhäuser* and *Lohengrin* a division of the music into separate numbers can still be quite easily discerned: it is in *Tristan* that the drama flows smoothly through uninterrupted music which appears to grow, indeed to generate spontaneously from the seed of the Prelude. The score's heavily sensuous chromaticism and the ecstatic richness of its orchestration combine to give the opera a curious psychological strength. In *Tristan und Isolde* Wagner has discovered for the first time how to reach simultaneously his

Stage design by Angelo Quaglio II for Act III of *Tristan und Isolde*.

Drawing of Wagner by Renoir
(above), based on a photograph
taken in 1867.

Liszt's daughter Cosima
(above right), in a drawing
by F. Preller, dated Weimar, 1855.

audience's conscious and subconscious responses. It must be emphasized, however, that this masterpiece of music-drama was composed to words which are occasionally even worse than his earlier libretti. In his review of the opera, the Viennese anti-Wagnerian critic Eduard Hanslick singled out the following passage:

> *Tristans Ehre – höchste Treu'*
> *Tristans Elend – kühnster Trotz*
> *Trug des Herzens, Traum der Ahnung;*
> *Ew'ger Trauer einz'ger Trost,*
> *Vergessens güt'ger Trank*
> *Dich trink' ich sonder Wank.*

> Tristan's honour – highest loyalty
> Tristan's anguish – keenest defiance
> Heart's deceit, wishful dreaming;
> Endless mourning the only consolation,
> Oblivion's kindly draught
> I drink thee unquestioningly.

Hanslick asked: 'Are there really connoisseurs who find this sort of thing poetic, profound or even German?' It is a fair question, though the only answer may be an evasion: whether poetic, profound or whether bombastic mediocrity, this is what Wagner the composer needed from Wagner the librettist in order to create one of the most remarkable operas ever written.

Wagner's position in Munich was fast becoming untenable. On 7 December 1865, no longer able to resist the pressure being put upon him by his ministers and by the police, who claimed that they could not be responsible for the composer's safety, Ludwig asked his beloved hero to leave the kingdom of Bavaria, at least for a few months. 'Though sundered, who can separate us?', he quoted from the *Götterdämmerung* libretto, as he bade Wagner farewell. Wagner, of course, was more concerned about losing the rich life which Ludwig made possible than losing the king's no doubt suffocating emotional friendship; and less concerned about losing Ludwig than Cosima who would not be able to travel openly with him. He left Munich with a very heavy heart. An additional shock had been the sudden death of the young tenor, Ludwig Schnorr. Schnorr had sung Tristan, and it was thought that the physical strain of the role may have contributed to his collapse.

The Signal in the Night, from Act II of *Tristan und Isolde*, pencil drawing by Henri Fantin-Latour, c. 1885. Fantin-Latour (1836–1904) was, like other Symbolist painters, greatly interested in Wagner and his work. This drawing of Isolde is one of Fantin-Latour's illustrations for *Richard Wagner*, a book by the music critic Adolphe Jullien, published in 1886.

The attacks on Wagner continued, even after he had left Munich. When it was charged that he had left his wife in penury, Minna, then within weeks of her death, wrote a public denial to the press, even though she now knew that her husband was the father of Cosima's child. Wagner heard the news of Minna's death while on his way to the French Riviera, which he had decided would be a desirable place to live. But by April he had changed his mind and, having refused an offer to go to America, he settled at the Villa Triebschen on Lake Lucerne. He had discovered the villa on Good Friday while he and Cosima were on an excursion to the lake. Built on a peninsula, the property contained a forest of poplars and was blessed with a panoramic view of the Alps. Poor besotted Ludwig paid the rent, Bertha the Viennese seamstress was engaged to look after the interior decoration which involved the use of an enormous amount of pink satin, and within a month Cosima and her three daughters, two of them her husband's, moved in with Wagner. The following month Ludwig wrote to say he intended to join Wagner at the Villa Triebschen as soon as he could arrange his abdication. Wagner was appalled, for Ludwig was of no use to him without his exchequer and his power. 'Out of love for me', he pleaded with Ludwig, 'remain amidst your people.' But Ludwig's messages were immediately followed up by Ludwig in person. Having himself announced as Walther von Stolzing, the romantic hero of *Die Meistersinger*, the twenty-four-year-old king appeared at the front door of the Villa Triebschen in order to be with the man he loved.

Earlier in their relationship, Wagner's response to Ludwig had been all that the youth could have wished. Visiting him daily 'like a sweetheart', Wagner would spend hours with the young man, lost,

Copy of a lost watercolour of the Villa Triebschen on Lake Lucerne, where Wagner and Cosima lived for many years.

Painting by Piloty of Ludwig II of Bavaria, 1865.

according to the composer, in mutual contemplation. It is only because of the frankness with which Wagner informed others of their relationship that one tends to surmise it was not physical. Now, with the strong-willed Cosima living with him, it was not so easy for Wagner to encourage the love-besotted Ludwig. Within two days the young king was back in Bavaria and facing a public outcry at his behaviour. But Ludwig's disillusionment with his friend had to be prevented. In a desperate attempt to convince Ludwig that his friendship with Cosima was purely platonic, Wagner and Cosima managed to persuade Cosima's not very strong-willed husband, Hans von Bülow, to spend the summer with them at Triebschen. They then appealed to Ludwig to write a letter to Bülow, complimenting him on the purity and nobility of his wife's character, and deploring the scurrilous gossip that was being circulated about her. (At this time, Cosima was pregnant with Wagner's second child!) Ludwig dutifully signed the letter, but it failed to have its full effect when made public, as the extraordinary prose style clearly revealed that it had been drafted by Wagner. Meanwhile, at Triebschen, Bülow had eyes and ears only for Wagner's genius, and none at all for Cosima's unfaithfulness.

Cosima's second child by Wagner, called Eva after the heroine of *Die Meistersinger*, was born on 17 February 1867. *Die Meistersinger* itself was revealed to the world on 21 June 1868. The victory of Prussia over the South German States and Austria in the Austro-Prussian War had brought about the downfall of those advisers of Ludwig who were most dangerous to Wagner, so the composer was able to return to Munich to supervise the production of his opera, which was conducted by Bülow. The première was an absolute triumph, the only unfortunate incident occurring when Wagner, who had sat consort-like beside the king in the royal box, stepped forward to acknowledge the applause. Bourgeois feeling in Munich was outraged.

In *Die Meistersinger*, Wagner turned aside from his preoccupation with the old myths, with the gods and goddesses of his *Ring* libretto, and with the symbolic personifications of *Tristan und Isolde*. To read the libretto of the opera, away from the music, is to realize that he was concerned, for once, to write about real people in a real, recognizable historical setting. For 'real', perhaps one should substitute 'realistic', for the fact that some of the characters in *Die Meistersinger von Nürnberg* are historical personages is quite beside the point.

Die Meistersinger von Nürnberg had its première in Munich on 21 June 1868. Shown here is the first scene of Act I, set in St Catherine's Church, where the young knight Walther von Stolzing contrives to meet Eva, daughter of the goldsmith Pogner.

Wagner's Hans Sachs does not claim to be based on the character, as far as it is known, of the historical Hans Sachs, Nuremberg poet and craftsman. The composer used the medieval Mastersingers' Guild and its members as pegs on which to build what he thought of as a splendid comedy. But his intransigent racial theories crept into the libretto, which might still have worked reasonably well as the basis of a light opera – what Wagner thought he was writing – had not his musical genius insisted on going its own way. No one coming to *Die Meistersinger* for the first time without any knowledge of German could possibly mistake it for the comedy which Wagner insisted it was. The sense of artistic discretion which was never one of his strongest attributes is considerably less evident in *Die Meistersinger* than in *Der fliegende Holländer* or even *Tristan und Isolde*. In a sense, Wagner the composer set to music the true libretto of *Die Meistersinger* that exists between the lines of the printed one: a hymn to artistic compromise with, in its final scene, an irrelevant aside appealing to the baser aspects of nationalism. The knight, Walther von Stolzing, begins as an artist answerable only to himself and his art. He is taught by the wise, kindly old Sachs how to curry the favour of his audience and thus win the hand of Eva by compromise, by giving the people what they want. 'Am stillen Herd' is the finer song, but it is 'Morgenlich leuchtend in rosigem Schein' which wins the prize in Act III.

The beginning of the chorus, 'Wach' auf', from Act III of *Die Meistersinger*, as reproduced in the Leipzig *Illustrirte Zeitung* in August 1868.

Heinrich Döll's design for the final
scene of *Die Meistersinger* at its
Munich première in 1868 (above).

Franz Seitz's costume designs for
Eva and Walther von Stolzing in
Die Meistersinger (right).

The blatant appeal to German nationalism of Hans Sachs's speech to the citizens of Nuremberg is a stunning example of Wagner the politician winning out over Wagner the artist. At the time of the opera's première it must have sounded like a clear invitation to launch a racial war against the impure Latins. Not only is 'heilige Deutsche Kunst' upheld as the great ideal, but the means of achieving and maintaining it are spelled out as clearly as Wagner elsewhere spelled out how to get rid of the Jews. The people, to whose judgment, as the libretto makes clear to us, art must in the end bow, are exhorted to obliterate the influence of French culture with its ephemeral and un-Germanic values: a project which was eventually to be implemented by Hitler, who also took action on one or two of Wagner's other hints. The passage that follows aroused that first Munich audience to a frenzy of enthusiasm, and led a Bayreuth audience in the thirties to rise to its feet and stand with hands raised in the Nazi salute throughout the chorus to the end of the opera two minutes later:

Oil painting, *Die Meistersinger von Nürnberg*, executed by Eduard Ille in 1866 and formerly in Schloss Berg on Lake Starnberg.

Hab't Acht! Uns dräuen üble Streich':
Zerfällt erst deutsches Volk und Reich,
In falscher wälscher Mäjestat
Kein Fürst bald mehr sein Volk versteht
Und wälschen Dunst mit wälschem Tand
Sie pflanzen uns in deutsches Land;
Was deutsch und echt, wüsst' keiner mehr,
Lebt's nicht in deutscher Meister Ehr'.
D'rum sag' ich euch: ehrt eure deutschen Meister!
Dann bannt ihr gute Geister;
Und gebt ihr ihrem Wirken Gunst,
Zerging' in Dunst
Das heil'ge röm'sche Reich,
Uns bleibe gleich
Die heil'ge deutsche Kunst!

Beware! Evil deeds are threatening us. Once the German people and kingdom have been submerged by false French majesty, soon no prince will understand his people, and they will plant ephemeral French taste and French vanity in German soil. What is German and true will no longer be recognized, unless it lives on in the honour of German masters. Therefore I say to you, honour your German masters. Then you will conjure up good spirits. And if you nourish their endeavours, though the Holy Roman Empire should dissolve into nothingness, holy German art would still remain to us.

There can be no denying that the music of Hans Sachs's great address is of an extraordinary emotive force, of the kind that was peculiarly Wagner's own and which has probably never been equalled by any other composer. The question that it presents is whether the nasty taste of the words is redeemed by the beauty and power of the music, or whether these very qualities render more dangerously effective a message which, left in Wagner's raw words, would surely have less appeal, for words speak primarily to the intellect and music to the emotions. It is a question which has never been satisfactorily answered, and one which is far removed from the comparatively simple matter of having to accept that artistic genius does not necessarily reside only in the breasts of those of the most impeccable moral purity.

One thing was now certain: Wagner could no longer stop the young man to whom he had written 'Deeply and from my heart I love no woman, no parents, no brother, no relations, no one but you' from realizing that he was being used. After the *Meistersinger* première, it was to be eight years before Wagner and Ludwig met again, though Ludwig continued to be faithful to his hero's artistic ideals and to support them generously. It was inevitable that Ludwig should have learned the truth, for Cosima gave birth to Wagner's

Cosima and her husband Richard Wagner.

third child in June 1869; the completely broken Hans von Bülow divorced her the following year, leaving Munich with the sarcastic laughter of his friends and colleagues ringing in his ears. There was now nothing to prevent the marriage of Richard and Cosima, which took place five weeks after Cosima's divorce.

Wagner was now at work on *Siegfried*, having completed the music of the earlier two *Ring* operas. Though the libretti of the four operas had been written in reverse order, the operas themselves had been composed in proper sequence. *Das Rheingold* had occupied Wagner in 1853–4, and *Die Walküre* in 1854–6. *Siegfried*, which he had begun in 1856, had been put aside while he worked on *Tristan und Isolde* for two years and *Die Meistersinger von Nürnberg* for five; he was not to finish it until 1871. The last work of the tetralogy, *Götterdämmerung*, was completed in 1874. Meanwhile, in 1870 at Triebschen, from musical material related to his work in progress, *Siegfried*, he composed the instrumental *Siegfried Idyll* as a Christmas present for his new wife and as a tribute to their latest child, Siegfried. It was played for the first time on the staircase at the villa on Christmas morning 1870, which was also Cosima's birthday.

RICHARD WAGNER. par GILL.

Engraving of the Vienna Opera-House (right), after a drawing by L. Rohbock, *c.* 1870.

Eduard Hanslick (1825–1904) (below right), an Austrian of Czech descent, was one of the most important and influential critics and music historians in nineteenth-century Vienna.

Cover of the Paris weekly, *L'Eclipse*, for 18 April 1869, with a caricature by Gill of Wagner attacking the eardrums of the public.

During these years at Triebschen, Wagner turned once again to the written word, and produced a number of essays and articles expounding his musical, political and racial theories. To the *Süddeutsche Presse* he contributed anonymously what was intended to form a series of fifteen articles called 'German Art and German Politics', expanding on the views expressed by Hans Sachs in *Die Meistersinger*. The shallow and degenerate French were contrasted with the vigorous and virtuous German race and its God-given mission: to civilize the world. In one of the articles, Wagner wrote a eulogy of Karl Sand, the murderer of the famous playwright Kotzebue, an insane student and disciple of the proto-Nazi Friedrich Ludwig Jahn. That such scurrilous articles could appear in a government newspaper began to worry even Ludwig. It was after the thirteenth article, in which Wagner wrote enthusiastically of Jahn's theory propagating the creation of a new nobility to be based on duty to the state, that Ludwig heeded the advice of his ministers and ordered publication of the articles to cease. When Wagner then

decided to reissue his notorious 'Jewishness in Music', even Cosima thought it indiscreet of him. But he was becoming increasingly obsessed with what he saw as the Jewish problem. As a recent biographer of Wagner has observed, the composer's reputation as an anti-Semite was so great that evil was suspected even where it was probably not intended. For instance, at the Viennese première of *Die Meistersinger* in February 1870, Beckmesser's serenade was hissed because it was believed to be a parody of synagogue chant: there were cries from the audience of 'We won't listen to it.' Wagner professed to consider this incident a Jewish insult to the authority of the Emperor Franz Josef. In fact, Wagner had based the character of Beckmesser on the Austrian music critic Eduard Hanslick, a noted anti-Wagnerian; in the first draft of the libretto, the character is called Hanslich (*sic*). Six years before the opera's première, Hanslick had been invited to hear Wagner read his libretto at the house of a Viennese physician. Hearing himself caricatured, Hanslick had fled from the house, to the amusement of the composer and his friends.

Title page of the first edition of Nietzsche's *The Birth of Tragedy from the Spirit of Music*, the first of his works to be published (above).

The philosopher Friedrich Nietzsche (1844–1900), photographed at about the time that Wagner first met him, *c.* 1868 (above right).

In 1868 Wagner had met the young philosopher, Friedrich Nietzsche, who, then aged twenty-four, was barely a year older than king Ludwig. As his influence over Ludwig waned, the composer began to concentrate on Nietzsche, whom he invited to Triebschen. The future author of *Thus Spake Zarathustra*, *Beyond Good and Evil* and *The Will to Power* was, therefore, early in his life privileged to observe at close range the will to power in action. Though Nietzsche, a professor of classical philosophy at the Swiss university of Basel, was still relatively unknown, Wagner tended to drop his name as though it resounded. Craving academic respectability – certainly his theories were sorely in need of it – the composer referred to Nietzsche and his colleague Erwin Rohde as 'my friends, the two university professors'.

During the years 1869 to 1871, when he was a constant visitor to Triebschen, Nietzsche was completely under the Wagner spell, and both husband and wife acted towards him as though the young philosopher's sole purpose in life was to be of use to them. Wagner realized that Nietzsche's intellect could be harnessed to establish the Wagnerian cause in the academic world, where so far it had not penetrated, the average Wagnerian being, as even the Master could

discern, a creature of emotion rather than of high intellectual capacity. When Nietzsche read Wagner the draft of his first book, *The Birth of Tragedy*, the composer was disappointed to discover that it was not about him, but about the Apollonian and Dionysian conflict in Greek drama. Nietzsche promptly made amends by interweaving a certain amount of Wagnerian polemic into his argument before publication. When the book appeared, it soon became evident that the academic establishment was not going to be won over to Wagner so easily. In fact, Nietzsche's career suffered a setback as a result, the general opinion being that Wagnerism was strictly for over-emotional women, homosexuals and anti-Semites.

Schopenhauer had been an early influence on Nietzsche, long before the young man became enthralled by Wagner as well. In *The Birth of Tragedy* Nietzsche's real difficulties lay not only in his attempt to reconcile the ideas of Schopenhauer with the artistic-political credo of Wagner, but also in his attempt to define precisely the nature of Schopenhauer's influence on Wagner. The irony of the situation was that it was through that most Dionysian of works, *Tristan und Isolde*, that the young Nietzsche found the inspiration to write *The Birth of Tragedy*, one of his most imaginative and truly creative books.

Wagner at the Villa Triebschen in 1868.

Engraving of *Das Rheingold* (left). At the top, the Rhinemaidens flee as Alberich seizes the gold; in the centre, the giants Fasolt and Fafner abduct Freia as ransom while the gods watch helplessly; below, Wotan and Loge descend to the depths of the Rhine to Nibelheim, where Alberich has made slaves of his brother Mime and the other Nibelungs.

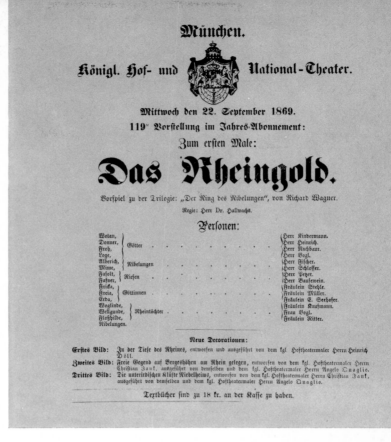

Towards the end of the close period of their relationship, Ludwig had asked Wagner to write a detailed account of his spiritual and physical life, a task which Wagner was only too happy to undertake. He dictated his memoirs to Cosima, but much of what he produced was closer to fiction than autobiography. Realizing that a great deal of *Mein Leben* would be at variance with statements and letters he had already written at various times, he attempted to call back much of his early correspondence. Even so, *Mein Leben* inadvertently remained too self-revelatory. After Wagner's death Cosima was to make her own alterations, softening many of his comments on other people.

Meanwhile, at Triebschen during 1868 and 1869, in addition to the dictation of *Mein Leben*, work continued on *Der Ring des Nibelungen*. The first opera, *Das Rheingold*, intended as a prelude to the other three, was produced in Munich on 22 September 1869. The events leading up to the première are decidedly bizarre, for Wagner, having first been enthusiastic about the proposed production, decided to regain power and influence for himself in Munich by sabotaging the performance. The conductor was to be Bülow's successor in Munich, the young and, as yet, relatively inexperienced Hans Richter. By ordering Richter to resign, on the grounds that the production had

Announcement of the première of *Das Rheingold* at the Imperial Court and National Theatre, Munich, on 22 September 1869. The playbill states that the décor for the first set, in the depths of the Rhine, was designed by Heinrich Döll and for the other two by Christian Jank and Angelo Quaglio.

The closing scene of *Das Rheingold* (right above). A rainbow bridge leads to Valhalla, the gods' new abode. As the others cross it, Loge remains behind, gazing into the Rhine.

The baritone Franz Betz (1835–1900) as Wotan (right below), the role he sang at the Bayreuth première of *Der Ring des Nibelungen* in 1876. Though Wagner would have preferred a bass for Wotan, he admired Betz's musicianship and settled for his lighter baritone timbre.

The bass-baritone Hans Hotter (b. 1908) as Wotan at Bayreuth in 1956 (far right, below). Hotter was Bayreuth's leading Wotan in the immediate post-war years. He also sang the role at Covent Garden, most notably in his own production in the early 1960s.

Sketch of the stage machinery at Bayreuth in 1876 (below), showing how the Rhinemaidens appeared to swim.

been badly organized and would discredit Wagner, the composer hoped and expected that Ludwig would then dismiss the theatre's administrator, Baron von Perfall, and install the conductor in his place. Wagner would then be able to rule through his puppet, Richter. Unfortunately the plan misfired. There were mishaps at the dress rehearsal, and Richter duly offered his indignant resignation. But the chief mechanist remedied the scenic mistakes without difficulty, and Ludwig was furious when he realized he was being made the dupe of his ex-hero. Richter was suspended, a new conductor was found for the postponed première one month later and Ludwig departed for one of his castles, remarking: 'J'en ai assez!'

When Wagner arrived in Munich, he found to his astonishment that he was refused admittance to the *Rheingold* rehearsals. There was nothing for him to do but return to Triebschen. The first performance of *Das Rheingold*, conducted by Franz Wüllner, took place in the absence of the composer. The official Wagnerites contrived for many years to keep alive the story that the Munich premières of *Das Rheingold* and *Die Walküre* were complete failures. The facts do not bear them out. The first performance of *Die Walküre* in Munich the following June, despite Wagner's attempts to dissuade his friends and admirers from attending it, was a triumphant success. Wagner's genius was now universally recognized by press and public, and the distinguished first-night audience, which included Brahms, Liszt, Saint-Saëns and Joachim, acclaimed the opera effusively. Wagner remained aloof at Triebschen.

Amalie Materna (1844–1918), the Austrian soprano (above), who began her career in Vienna as a soubrette in operetta, but later became a dramatic soprano. She created the role of Brünnhilde at the Bayreuth première of the *Ring* and in 1882 was the first Kundry in *Parsifal*.

The bass Joseph Nierung as Hunding at Bayreuth in 1876 (above right).

One of the most admired Brünnhildes in the 1920s and 1930s was the Norwegian soprano Kirsten Flagstad (1895–1962), seen here in *Die Walküre* (right).

In Act II of *Die Walküre* (above left), Brünnhilde appears before Siegmund to announce that he will die in the fight with Hunding. Sieglinde, who has fled with Siegmund from Hunding's hut, lies sleeping by his side. In Act III (below left), Brünnhilde rescues Sieglinde after Siegmund's death and brings her to her sister Valkyries, who flee in alarm at the approach of Wotan, their father.

Three weeks after the première of *Die Walküre*, the Franco-Prussian War broke out. One would expect Wagner's sympathies to be with Prussia, but there is something almost obscene in the glee with which he greeted the defeat of France. It inspired him to write not only a poem, 'To the German Army Before Paris', a piece of jingoistic doggerel, but, even worse, an anonymous play ridiculing the sufferings of the starving during the siege of Paris, which he wanted set to Offenbach-style music. Having dealt with the French, he then turned to the composition of a *Kaisermarsch* to celebrate the Prussian victory.

By 1871 Wagner had come to the conclusion that his works would never be staged as he wanted them to be until he could control a theatre of his own, a theatre so designed that it would both project his imaginative creations and, in turn, inspire them. Further thought on this subject led him to decide that a theatre would have to be specially built, in which *Der Ring des Nibelungen* could be staged, not as part of the ordinary operatic repertory of a busy theatre, but under the ideal conditions which such a huge and unique work required.

Caricature of the Prussian statesman Otto von Bismarck (1815–98). Wagner at first admired Bismarck and sent him the jingoistic poem he had written to celebrate the German victory over France in 1870. But when Bismarck, as head of the German Reichstag, granted equality of citizenship to the Jews, Wagner became violently opposed to him.

Richard and Cosima Wagner in 1872.

Vienna in 1872, as depicted by Franz Alt, showing the corner of the Ring and the Kärnterstrasse with the newly built opera-house. In 1875 Wagner gave five concerts in Vienna to raise funds for the building of his Festival Theatre at Bayreuth and also rehearsed the Vienna productions of *Tannhäuser* and *Lohengrin*.

The Wagner theatre in Munich which he and Ludwig had once planned together was now never likely to exist, so the composer began to look elsewhere, both for finance and for an actual site. Eventually his choice fell upon the small Bavarian town of Bayreuth.

Wagner and as many of his supporters as could be mustered then began the task of stimulating local Bayreuth interest in the idea of developing the town as a centre of Wagnerian music-drama. Having gained the goodwill of the mayor of Bayreuth and one or two influential citizens, Wagner began fund-raising in earnest. Even Nietzsche joined enthusiastically in procuring subscribers, and a thousand 300-thaler shares were issued. The site, an excellent one on a small hilltop just outside the town, was donated by the Bayreuth municipality, and king Ludwig was yet again persuaded to part with a sum of money to enable Wagner to build a suitable residence for himself and his family in the town. A temporary theatre was to be erected, based on designs previously prepared for the abortive Munich theatre. In 1874 the Wagners left Triebschen and moved to Bayreuth. But the subscription scheme failed and at the last moment Wagner had to appeal once more to Ludwig, for the entire enterprise was already so heavily in debt that, unless a large amount of money could immediately be raised, it would collapse. Ludwig was understandably reluctant to come yet again to Wagner's aid, but when the composer made it clear that the Bayreuth scheme could not proceed without him, the king instructed his finance minister to negotiate a loan. Thus the theatre was saved. The temporary structure opened in 1876 with a complete performance of the four operas of *The Ring* on 13, 14, 16 and 17 August. That temporary structure is still in use as the Festival Theatre, where Wagner's operas are performed every summer.

Front page of the humorous weekly paper *Kikeriki*, 1875, with a cartoon feature depicting a Wagner concert. Evidently the sounds of Wagner's orchestra were thought by the cartoonist to be distinctly disharmonious.

Zum Richard Wagner-Konzert.

Der Erfolg war außerordentlich — dies schicken wir voraus. Wie ungleich großartiger würde sich derselbe aber erst gestaltet haben, wenn die Instrumentenmacher gleichen Schritt mit den Ideen des Meisters zu halten verstünden! Denn Eines steht fest: Richard Wagner braucht auch neue Klänge; Klänge, die sich dem jetzt in Gebrauch befindlichen Material nicht entlocken lassen. Es bleibt daher nichts übrig, als daß Kikeriki wieder seine Erfinderhose anzieht.

Nehmen wir beispielsweise an, man hätte ihm diese Monstre-Harfe zur Verfügung gestellt! Wie ganz anders wäre stellenweise die Wirkung gewesen!

Eine Katze, deren Bauch man mit dem Fiedelbogen streicht, müßte in der Instrumentation von Klageliedern eben so gut zu verwenden sein

Das rapide Geklirre, womit Wagner gerne den Zusammenbruch irgend einer Seele ausdrückt, wäre durch das Ausleeren von Glasscherben gewiß ganz gut zu imitiren,

Gewisse schrille Töne, wie sie Richard Wagner in seinen Schöpfungen braucht, ließen sich doch so leicht mittelst schartiger Messer alten Porzellantellern entlocken.

wie der empfindliche Jagdhund, welcher den Ton einer Kindertrompete nicht verträgt, und daher mit seinem Jammer bis in's hohe C hinaufgeht.

während endlich gewisse Aufschreie und temperamentvolle Quitschlaute sicherlich auf obige Weise zu Stande gebracht werden könnten.

97

The Villa Wahnfried (right),
the house which Wagner had built
for himself and Cosima in Bayreuth
and which was paid for by
Ludwig II. The mural over the
entrance (above) was designed by
Robert Krausse.

The exterior (above left) and the
interior (below left) of the
Festival Theatre at Bayreuth, which
opened on 13 August 1876.

Drawings by Knut Ekwall based on the first production of the *Ring* operas at Bayreuth and published in the Leipzig *Illustrirte Zeitung* of 16 and 30 September 1876: the Rhinemaidens admiring the gold in the depths of the river in the first scene of *Das Rheingold* (above), and the death of Siegmund, speared by Hunding while Sieglinde watches helplessly, in Act II of *Die Wälkure* (above right).

The four music-dramas of *The Ring*, which ideally should be heard complete and consecutively, demand a greater degree of concentration from the listener than any other opera by Wagner, or by anyone else. This is not simply because of the vast system of nearly two hundred *leitmotifs* woven into the giant work, but because of the complex nature of the ideas inherent in it, and of the variety of interpretations to which it is susceptible. Considered as an old Norse saga of gods, heroes, dwarfs, dragons and giants, reworked by Wagner into frequently bad and occasionally repetitive verse, and then set to music which veers between the sublime and the ridiculous, *The Ring* is obviously a flawed and unsatisfactory affair. But its power to move an audience lies elsewhere, in Wagner's ability to

bypass his listeners' intellectual and aesthetic responses and to communicate directly with the deepest recesses of the psyche. The naïve absurdities of the plot, the antiquated trappings of the old saga, all fade into insignificance before the power of Wagner's music. In a sense, *The Ring* fails as a vindication of its composer's theory of the *Gesamtkunstwerk*, for its message is delivered by the music alone: not even by the voices to any significant extent, but by Wagner's orchestration. Whether *The Ring* is successful as theatre or as music-drama is debatable. What is beyond question is that it provides the listener with a great musical experience, and one that in some mysterious way transcends the art of music alone to become almost a spiritual or psychical experience.

Two more drawings by Knut Ekwall from the Leipzig *Illustrirte Zeitung*: the awakening of the sleeping Brünnhilde by the young hero in Act III of *Siegfried* (above left), and Siegfried's funeral procession in Act III of *Götterdämmerung* (above).

Among the distinguished audience which assembled in Bayreuth in 1876 was Tchaikovsky, whose description of the occasion appeared in a Russian magazine:

The town was in a state of great excitement. Crowds of people, natives and strangers, were gathered together from the four corners of the earth, and all rushed to the railway station to see the Emperor arrive. I witnessed the show from the window of a house near by. First, some magnificent uniforms passed by, then a procession of the musicians from the Wagner theatre, led by their conductor Hans Richter, then the fascinating figure of the Abbé Liszt with that fine characteristic head of his, which one has so often admired in portraits. Finally, in a splendid carriage, the serene old man, Richard Wagner himself, with his aquiline nose and his slightly ironic smile. . . . During the Festival itself, food was the main interest of the public, the performances themselves taking second place. Cutlets, baked potatoes, omelettes are much more enthusiastically discussed than the music of Wagner.

Tchaikovsky did not respond favourably to *The Ring*, finding *Das Rheingold* 'absolute nonsense, from a musical point of view' and expressing grave doubts as to the validity of Wagner's operatic principles. His doubts have since been echoed by several generations of musicians, critics and music-lovers, yet so far the tetralogy has survived. Though it may not be the artistic equal of *Der fliegende Holländer*, *Lohengrin* and *Tristan und Isolde*, *Der Ring des Nibelungen* is, for all its unevenness and disproportionate length and shape, the composer's most important work, considered in extra-musical, indeed extra-aesthetic terms. It is certainly the work on which most critical theories of Wagner are based. It is also the one in which Wagner's method of identifying characters and situations with *leitmotifs* is most consistently adopted.

Such is the power and emotive force of Wagner's music in certain parts of *The Ring* that one is inclined to forgive and forget the garrulity and tedium of others. Such, too, are the scale and nature of the vast enterprise that it is possible to interpret *The Ring* in terms of sociology, politics, economics, history, psychology or moral philosophy. It would be as unfair to blame the composer for the fanatical enthusiasm with which Nazi Germany adopted him and his *Übermensch* Siegfried as the embodiment of their ideals, as it would to ignore the distinct probability that Wagner himself would have been delighted by the adulation of Adolf Hitler. The fervent keepers of the flame in twentieth-century Bayreuth certainly referred to Wagner in the Festival programmes of the 1930s as a spiritual member of the Nazi Party, and compared the advent of Hitler to Parsifal's final act of redemption.

The Ring, then, is not a work to be dismissed or accepted lightly.

Winifred Wagner, the composer's
English daughter-in-law, at
Bayreuth in 1931 with Wilhelm
Furtwängler and Arturo Toscanini,
both seated (above). This was the
only year in which these two great
conductors both appeared at
Bayreuth, for they quarrelled and
Toscanini left Bayreuth, never to
return. Furtwängler himself resigned
the following year after a dispute
with Winifred, who was by then
artistic director of the Festival.

Winifred Wagner greeting Adolf
Hitler at Bayreuth, 1939 (left).

Georg Unger (1837–87), the German tenor who created the role of Siegfried at Bayreuth in 1876 and is thus the first Wagner *Heldentenor* (right).

Ernst Kraus (1863–1941) as Siegfried and Hans Breuer (1868–1929) as Mime, two tenors who had distinguished careers at Bayreuth (far right). Between 1899 and 1909, Kraus was the outstanding Bayreuth Siegfried, while Breuer sang Mime there every year between 1896 and 1914.

Lauritz Melchior (1890–1973), the Danish tenor, as Siegfried in 1928 (below right). During the 1920s and 1930s he sang this and other Wagnerian roles at Bayreuth, Berlin, Covent Garden and the Metropolitan, New York.

Paul Richter as Siegfried in Fritz Lang's film *Siegfrieds Tod*, a silent version of the old Norse myth, made in 1923 (far right, below).

George Bernard Shaw (1856–1950), the famous playwright and critic, and author of *The Perfect Wagnerite*, an important book on Wagner's *Ring*, which interprets the operas in terms of nineteenth-century economic theory.

A useful key to its understanding lies in Bernard Shaw's *The Perfect Wagnerite*. Shaw, having noted that at the point where *The Ring* changes from music-drama into opera, it also ceases to be philosophic and becomes didactic, continues:

The philosophic part is a dramatic symbol of the world as Wagner observed it. In the didactic part, the philosophy degenerates into the prescription of a romantic nostrum for all human ills. Wagner, only mortal after all, succumbed to the panacea mania when his philosophy was exhausted, like any of the rest of us.

In this particular weakness lies his similarity to Shaw the playwright-politician-philosopher.

By the time of the *Ring* première, Wagner's disciple Nietzsche had become disillusioned with the Master, having seen the artist inexorably giving way to the political opportunist. The vulgarly philistine atmosphere of Bayreuth confirmed Nietzsche's doubts, and it was the paranoiac anti-Semitism of the Wagner supporters that acted as the final straw. The ways of the two geniuses now lay along uncompromisingly different paths.

Richard and Cosima with their son Siegfried, born at Triebschen on 6 June 1869 (right).

Eva, Siegfried, Isolde, Daniela and Blandine dressed to play Wagnerian roles (left). Only Daniela and Blandine had to change their names – to Senta and Elisabeth.

Wagner's son Siegfried as young Siegfried (below left) in the original costume of 1876, and his daughter Isolde in the original 1886 costume for Isolde (below).

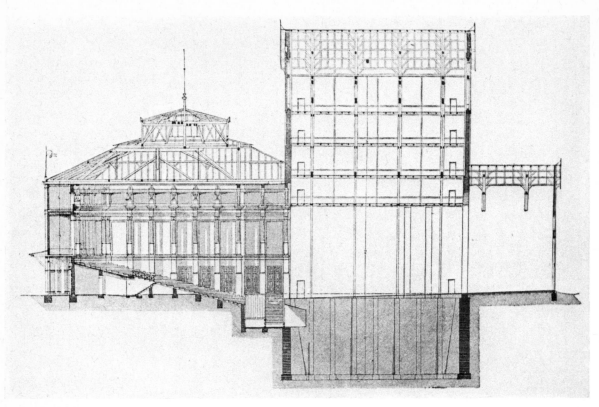

Two views of the Bayreuth Festival Theatre: an architectural sectional drawing (left) and a drawing of an orchestral rehearsal by a member of the orchestra (below left).

Judith Gautier-Mendès in 1875 (above), daughter of the famous poet Théophile Gautier and Wagner's lover in the early Bayreuth years.

The financial failure of the Bayreuth performances of 1876 forced Wagner to return to the life of a touring conductor for he needed to raise funds to reduce a large deficit. A Wagner festival of twenty concerts was planned for the Royal Albert Hall in London, but only eight were given, increasing Wagner's overdraft still further. The following year, Ludwig II came once again to the aid of Bayreuth. Wagner's liabilities were transferred to the state of Bavaria under certain conditions, one of which was that his new opera, *Parsifal*, whose libretto had now been completed, should be performed only at Bayreuth, and 'never desecrated by contact with any profane stage'.

Wagner, now in somewhat failing health, devoted himself to the composition of *Parsifal*. At the same time he embarked on the last of his love-affairs, with Judith Gautier, daughter of Théophile Gautier and wife of the Jewish poet and critic Catulle Mendès. Cosima, more diplomatic than her predecessor, Minna, made no difficulties. Partly at the Villa Wahnfried in Bayreuth, partly in Italy, the music of *Parsifal* was slowly urged into existence, its composer swathed in his indispensable silks and satins, sprinkled with exotic perfumes. By January 1882 the opera was complete and fully scored. Six months later, on 26 July, it was given its first performance at Bayreuth.

Three Jews who worked on the Christian drama *Parsifal*, which had its première at Bayreuth in 1882: from left to right, Paul von Joukowsky (décor), Hermann Levi (conductor) and Karl Brandt (stage manager).

Ludwig II's chief conductor was now Hermann Levi, the son of a rabbi. Wagner, furious that Ludwig had apparently rejected the anti-Semitic message of *Parsifal*, attempted with the utmost passion to turn Ludwig against Levi. Ludwig's comment that religious and racial differences were unimportant compared with the essential brotherhood of mankind was an especially bitter blow to the composer, who had no alternative but to accept Levi, for whose musical ability he had nothing but the highest praise, as the conductor of *Parsifal*. Official tolerance of Jews, however, he regarded as certain to bring about Germany's ruin: he professed himself appalled that they were now allowed full citizenship, fearing that they would soon 'consider themselves in every conceivable respect to be Germans, just as Negroes in Mexico are encouraged to regard themselves as white'.

Ludwig had defied Wagner to the point of insisting that, unless Levi were to conduct, there would be no performance of *Parsifal*. Wagner now resorted to other tactics: he made himself personally so offensive to Levi that the conductor asked to be relieved of the task of conducting *Parsifal*, and had to be coaxed back. Finally, when he realized he was defeated, Wagner wrote to Ludwig disingenuously agreeing that he would accept Levi as conductor of *Parsifal* without

Two designs by Paul von
Joukowsky for the 1882
performance of *Parsifal* at Bayreuth:
Kundry's costume in Act II (left)
and the staging of the final scene
(below).

enquiring into his religion! When the king's response indicated his distaste for racial intolerance (his new soulmate was the twenty-four-year-old Austrian Jewish actor, Josef Kainz), Wagner spewed forth a foul letter in which he informed Ludwig that he considered the Jewish race to be 'the born enemies of pure Mankind and all that is noble in it'. It was against this background that Hermann Levi conducted the first performances of Wagner's sacred Christian drama, *Parsifal*.

It is possible to view *Parsifal* merely as sickly, *fin de siècle* homo-erotic fantasy, an immensely long and slow-moving opera whose length is extraordinarily disproportionate to its musical and dramatic worth. On the surface, it is a work of pious Christianity, though, as the American Wagner critic Robert W. Gutman has pointed out, Wagner detested Christianity which he saw as 'Judaic error per-petuated'. But *Parsifal*, whatever else it is, is a complex work of art. If it can be seen as a disgraceful attempt to give aesthetic validity to the violent racial prejudice of his contemporaneous articles and essays in the *Bayreuther Blätter*, it can also be seen as the portrait of a soul on its journey towards maturity. But whether it is a 'brooding nightmare of Aryan anxiety' (Gutman's phrase) or a celebration of high-minded homosexuality, *Parsifal* seems now very much of its time, much more so than *Tristan und Isolde*, than *The Ring* or *Die Meister-singer*. Parsifal's purity was threatened both racially and sexually. Is it fanciful to trace a connection, as Gutman has done, between Par-sifal's monastic homosexuality and 'the not dissimilar fellowship of Ernst Röhm's troopers'? The simplistic answer is to say that art is art, life is life, and never the twain shall meet. But *Parsifal* surely deserves to be considered less simplistically than this. Allowing of fewer varieties of interpretation than *The Ring*, it has nevertheless been subjected to many, by critics desirous either of emphasizing Wagner's anti-Semitism or of diverting attention from it.

A study of the opera's libretto, in relation to Wagner's various prose writings, makes it clear that the composer-dramatist's concern was to 'Aryanize' Christianity by divorcing it from its Jewish beginnings. In his essay 'Heldentum und Christentum' (Heroism and Christianity), written in 1881 as a polemical appendage to *Parsifal*, he explains how the Aryans, the Teutonic leaders of mankind, sprang from the gods, only the lesser races being descended from the apes. Christianity's worship of a Jewish tribal God, made flesh in the Jewish Christ, appalled him. In *Parsifal* he re-created Christ in his own Wagnerian, Gentile image. Parsifal is an Aryan Christ, though in another essay, 'Religion and Art', Wagner voiced his own very strong doubts as to the Jewishness of the original Jesus. In the same essay, God is taken to task, not only for being Jewish

The 1882 production of *Parsifal* at Bayreuth: Gurnemanz, Kundry and Parsifal (above right) and Kundry in Act II (far right, above).

Klingsor's magic garden in Act II of *Parsifal* (below right). Max Brückner's oil painting is based on Paul von Joukowsky's designs for the Bayreuth première.

Two interpretations of the Grail Temple for the production of *Parsifal* at Bayreuth: a design by Wieland Wagner from the 1930s (far right, above) and Paul von Joukowsky's design, which was used at Bayreuth from 1882 to 1933, as depicted in Max Brückner's oil painting (far right, below).

Wieland Wagner, Adolf Hitler and Wolfgang Wagner, photographed at Bayreuth, *c.* 1935 (right).

but also for being anti-vegetarian. (Hitler was to carry Wagner's Aryanization of Christ a stage further, declaring him to have been the son of a Greek soldier in the Roman army of occupation!) Klingsor in *Parsifal*, Wagner informed Cosima, represented not only the tainted blood of the Jew, but also the Jesuit. The luxurious garden of Jewish art, Jewish voluptuousness, is made to disappear by the magical power of the Aryan cross. In the third act of the opera, the pure blood of the Aryan Jesus glows with desire to rejoin the blood in the sacred cup. Amfortas, who had allowed his blood to mingle with that of the racially inferior Kundry, is redeemed, while Kundry is reduced to that menial grovelling which is her proper condition.

The music of *Parsifal* is, at least intermittently, as powerful and compelling as anything Wagner ever composed. To those who cosily and sentimentally equate great art with great morality, the opera stands as an uncomfortable reminder that art and morality are really not on speaking terms. Nietzsche described *Parsifal* as 'a work of malice, of vindictiveness . . . a bad work . . . an outrage on morality'. He also recognized the power, indeed the beauty, of much of its music. But, if the arts can influence human behaviour, then presumably they can influence it in a number of directions. One is inclined to believe that music itself is essentially innocent, and that only when it is allied to text or drama can it corrupt. However, corruption is itself a question-begging concept: perhaps it is safer to declare that, to some temperaments, *Parsifal* is an uncommonly persuasive work of art.

The Palazzo Vendramin in Venice (above), where Wagner lived from September 1882 until his death in February 1883.

After the *Parsifal* performances at Bayreuth, Wagner and Cosima left for Venice, where they occupied part of the duke of Grazia's splendid fifteenth-century Palazzo Vendramin. Wagner's heart was in a weak condition, and the fights he was having with Cosima over a lady whom he wished to include in the following year's *Parsifal* performances must have seriously exacerbated his state of general ill-health. On 13 February 1883, after a slight heart attack, he retired to bed to work on an essay, 'The Feminine Element in Humanity'. While Cosima was at lunch, Wagner's bell began to ring violently. She hastened to him, and he died shortly afterwards in her arms.

Wagner has lived on, both as the controversial figurehead of a clique, and as an indisputably great composer of opera. That his racial and other theories were either evil or absurd or both is irrelevant to his stature as an artist. In his own day, and immediately after his death, he was a very influential artist, though his influence is apparent less in the work of other composers than in that of poets and painters. Those composers whose operas can be called Wagnerian (Humperdinck, Reyer) are not of the first rank, with the exception of Debussy, whose *Pelléas et Mélisande* is deeply indebted to Wagner, and to *Parsifal* in particular: but there is hardly a major poet of the turn of

Portrait drawing of Wagner by Paul von Joukowsky (right), inscribed by Cosima, 'R. reading 12 Febr. 1883'.

R. Wagner
13 Feb. 1883.

Evocation of Erda (far right) from
Act III of *Siegfried*, a pencil
drawing by Henri Fantin-Latour,
c. 1885.

the century who did not walk in the valley of the shadow of the
Master. In Paris, the Symbolists came under his sway. French poets
such as Gérard de Nerval and Théophile Gautier were enthusiastic
Wagnerians, and both Baudelaire and Mallarmé wrote essays on the
composer. The Symbolists were impressed as much with Wagner's
polemics as with his music, especially with his references to the
relationship of poetry to music. Wagnerian references abound in the
art of the time: Cézanne painted an *Overture to Tannhäuser*, Renoir
painted the composer's portrait, and artists such as Fantin-Latour,
Odilon Redon and, in England, Whistler and Aubrey Beardsley
produced lithographs of scenes from Wagner operas.

Of course, the Wagner influence extended to other composers.
Richard Strauss, César Franck and Saint-Saëns are names which
come immediately to mind. But it is in his tone-poems rather than his
operas, except the first, *Guntram*, that Strauss reveals the extent of his
debt to Wagner. The Wagner music-dramas have failed to exercise
a lasting influence on the art form of opera, though they are themselves
among the most important works of art in the nineteenth century.
Wagner's only peers as creators of opera are Mozart in the preceding
century and his own contemporary, Verdi. It may be necessary to
overcome a distaste for Wagner the man in order to appreciate
Wagner the composer, but anyone who fails to conquer such a
distaste cuts himself off from the work of a major artist, surely the
greatest of the nineteenth-century romantics, and the creator of music
of unique emotive power and compulsion.

Wagner's grave in the garden of the
Villa Wahnfried at Bayreuth.

CHRONOLOGY

1813 Wagner born on 22 May in Leipzig.

1814 His mother marries Ludwig Geyer in August, and the family moves to Dresden.

1821 Geyer dies in September.

1827 The family moves to Leipzig.

1829 First compositions, juvenilia, mainly for piano.

1831 Studies music with Weinlig.

1832 Begins work on first opera, *Die Hochzeit*. Text completed, but composition abandoned.

1833 Begins work on *Die Feen* in August. Opera completed the following January but not staged until 1888, after his death.

1834 Writes text of *Das Liebesverbot*. Engaged as conductor at Magdeburg.

1836 Completes music of *Das Liebesverbot*, which is performed in Magdeburg under his direction. In November, marries Minna Planer.

1837 Engaged as conductor in Riga.

1838 Begins work on *Rienzi*.

1839 Leaves Riga for Paris.

1840 Finishes *Rienzi*, begins work on *Der fliegende Holländer*.

1841 Finishes *Der fliegende Holländer*.

1842 First performance of *Rienzi* in Dresden. Begins *Tannhäuser* libretto.

1843 Becomes *Kapellmeister* at the Dresden Opera. First performance of *Der fliegende Holländer* in Dresden under his direction.

1844 Writes music of *Tannhäuser*.

1845 Scoring of *Tannhäuser* completed by April. First performance of *Tannhäuser* in Dresden, conducted by Wagner.

1847 Works on *Lohengrin*.

1848 His mother dies. Completes *Lohengrin*, and writes libretto, 'Siegfrieds Tod', in due course to become *Götterdämmerung*.

1849 Liszt produces *Tannhäuser* in Weimar. Wagner goes into political exile, settles in Zürich.

1850 First performance of *Lohengrin* under Liszt in Weimar.

1851 Continues work on what is to become the libretto of the *Ring* tetralogy.

1852 Meets the Wesendonks.

1853 Text of *Der Ring des Nibelungen* privately printed. Begins work on music of *Das Rheingold*.

1854 Finishes *Das Rheingold*, begins *Die Walküre*.

1856 *Die Walküre* completed, *Siegfried* begun.

1857 *Siegfried* abandoned in the middle of the second act. Libretto of *Tristan und Isolde* written, and music begun.

1858 Wesendonk Lieder, begun previous year, now completed. Continues work on *Tristan und Isolde*.

1859 *Tristan und Isolde* completed.

1860 In Paris, adapts *Tannhäuser* for performance at the Paris Opéra.

1861 Paris production of *Tannhäuser*. Minna leaves him. Writes libretto of *Die Meistersinger von Nürnberg*.

1862 Begins composition of *Die Meistersinger*.

1863 Relationship with Cosima von Bülow develops.

1864 Friendship with Ludwig II of Bavaria begins.

1865 A daughter, Isolde, born to Wagner and Cosima. He resumes composition of *Siegfried*. First performance of *Tristan und Isolde* in Munich, conducted by Hans von Bülow.

1866 Death of Minna Wagner. Cosima leaves her husband to live with Wagner at the Villa Triebschen on Lake Lucerne.

1867 A daughter, Eva, born to Wagner and Cosima. *Die Meistersinger* completed.

1868 Wagner meets the young Nietzsche. First performance of *Die*

Meistersinger in Munich under von Bülow.

1869 *Götterdämmerung* begun. First performance of *Das Rheingold* in Munich. Birth of Wagner and Cosima's third child, Siegfried.

1870 Cosima divorced by von Bülow, marries Wagner. First performance of *Die Walküre* in Munich. Memoirs, *Mein Leben*, printed privately. *Siegfried Idyll* composed.

1871 *Siegfried* completed.

1872 Foundation-stone of Festival Theatre laid.

1874 *Götterdämmerung* completed. Wagner and Cosima settle in Bayreuth.

1876 Opening of the Bayreuth Festival Theatre with the first complete performance of *Der Ring des Nibelungen* under Richter.

1877 Writes libretto of *Parsifal*.

1879 Composition of *Parsifal* completed.

1880 In Italy.

1882 First performance of *Parsifal* under Levi at Bayreuth.

1883 Wagner dies in Venice on 13 February and is buried at Bayreuth on 18 February.

SELECT BIBLIOGRAPHY

DONINGTON, Robert *Wagner's 'Ring'* (1963)
ELLIS, William Ashton *Life of Richard Wagner* (6 vols 1900–08)
KREHBIEL, Edward Henry *Studies in the Wagnerian Drama* (1898)
LAVIGNAC, Albert *The Music-Dramas of Richard Wagner* (1898)
NEWMAN, Ernest *Wagner as Man and Artist* (1924)
MAGEE, Brian *Aspects of Wagner* (1968)
NEWMAN, Ernest *Wagner Nights* (1949)
GUTMAN, Robert W. *Richard Wagner* (1968)
SHAW, George Bernard *The Perfect Wagnerite* (2nd ed. 1903)
STEIN, Jack M. *Richard Wagner and the Synthesis of the Arts* (1960)
STEIN, Leon *The Racial Thinking of Richard Wagner* (1950)
WAGNER, Richard *Gesammelte Schriften* (10 vols 1871–5; English trans. *Richard Wagner's Prose Works* 8 vols 1892–9)
— *Mein Leben* (2 vols 1911; English trans. *My Life* 1911)
WAGNER, Siegfried *Erinnerungen* (1923)
WAGNER, Wieland (ed.) *Richard Wagner und das neue Bayreuth* (1962)
WESTERNHAGEN, Curt von *Richard Wagner; Sein Werk, sein Wesen, seine Welt* (1956)
WOLZOGEN, Hans von *Erinnerungen an Richard Wagner* (n.d.)

LIST OF ILLUSTRATIONS

Half-title page: First page of the orchestral sketch for Act III of *Tristan und Isolde*, Lucerne, 1 May 1859. Richard Wagner Archiv, Bayreuth.

Frontispiece: Richard Wagner (1813–83). Chalk drawing by Franz von Lenbach, *c.* 1874. Photo Radio Times Hulton Picture Library.

5 Brühl in Leipzig, with Wagner's birthplace on the left. Watercolour, 1840. Museum für Geschichte der Stadt Leipzig.

6 Ludwig Geyer (1779–1821). Self-portrait in oils, *c.* 1806. Richard Wagner Gedenkstätte der Stadt Bayreuth.

Johanna Rosine Wagner (1774–1848). Oil painting by Ludwig Geyer, 1813. Richard Wagner Gedenkstätte der Stadt Bayreuth.

7 St Thomas's Churchyard, Leipzig. Coloured lithograph. Museum für Geschichte der Stadt Leipzig.

8 Carl Maria von Weber (1786–1826) at Covent Garden. Lithograph by John Hayter, 1826. Royal College of Music, London.

9 Rosalie Wagner (1803–37), Richard's sister. Photo Radio Times Hulton Picture Library.

10 Adolf Wagner (1774–1835), Richard's uncle. Drawing, 1832. Nationalarchiv der Richard-Wagner-Stiftung, Bayreuth.

11 Wilhelmine Schröder-Devrient (1804–60). Engraving after Beritze, nineteenth century. Photo Festspiele Bildarchiv, Bayreuth.

13 Title page of the compositional sketch for *Die Feen*. Richard Wagner Archiv, Bayreuth.

Closing scene of *Die Feen* at the Munich performance of 29 June 1888. Wood engraving after a drawing by Gottfried Franz. *Illustrirte Zeitung*, Leipzig, 28 December 1889.

14 Felix Mendelssohn-Bartholdy (1809–47). Photo Radio Times Hulton Picture Library.

15 Vincenzo Bellini (1801–35). Radio Times Hulton Picture Library.

16 Silhouette of Wagner by an unknown artist, Magdeburg, 1835. The Burrell Collection, Curtis Institute of Music, Philadelphia.

17 Minna Planer (1809–66). Photograph. Photo Radio Times Hulton Picture Library.

19 Title page of the text of *Das Liebesverbot*, endorsed by the censor's office in Magdeburg, 17 March 1836. Richard Wagner Gedenkstätte der Stadt Bayreuth.

21 Finale of Act II of *Rienzi*, performed in 1843 with Joseph Tichatschek (1807–86) as Rienzi. Watercolour by Baron von Leyser. Theatermuseum, Munich.

23 Giacomo Meyerbeer (1791–1864). Lithograph. Richard Wagner Gedenkstätte der Stadt Bayreuth.

25 Façade of the Paris Opéra, rue le Peletier, before the fire of 1873. Photo Roger Viollet.

26 Hector Berlioz (1803–69). Portrait in oils by Gustave Courbet, *c.* 1860. Louvre, Paris. Photo Giraudon.

28 Richard and Minna Wagner in Paris. Caricature by E.B. Kietz, 1840–1. Richard Wagner Archiv, Bayreuth.

30–31 Sketches of the cast for the première of *Rienzi*: Joseph Tichatschek as Rienzi; Henriette Wüst as Irene; Wilhelmine Schröder-Devrient as Adriano; Paul Dettmer as Colonna; Michael Wächter as Orsini. *Illustrirte Zeitung*, Leipzig, 12 August 1843.

32 Exterior of the Court Theatre, Dresden. Hand-coloured lithograph, *c.* 1841. Richard Wagner Museum, Triebschen.

Interior of the Court Theatre, Dresden. Coloured lithograph. Richard Wagner Archiv, Bayreuth.

33 Wilhelmine Schröder-Devrient. Lithograph by Hanfstaengl, 1840. Photo Radio Times Hulton Picture Library.

34 Final scene of Act IV of *Rienzi*, at the Dresden première, 20 October 1842. *Illustrirte Zeitung*, Leipzig, 12 August 1843.

36 Richard Wagner in middle life. Portrait by Jager. Photo Radio Times Hulton Picture Library.

37 Theatre poster for the première of *Der fliegende Holländer* at Dresden, 2 January 1843.

38 Drawings of the cast at the Dresden première of *Der fliegende Holländer*: Michael Wächter as the Dutchman; Wilhelmine Schröder-

Devrient as Senta; Herr Reinhold as Erik. *Illustrirte Zeitung*, Leipzig, 7 October 1843.

Final scene of *Der fliegende Holländer*. *Illustrirte Zeitung*, Leipzig, 7 October 1843.

39 The Steersman's Song from *Der fliegende Holländer*. *Illustrirte Zeitung*, Leipzig, 15 July 1843.

41 Emmy Destinn (1878–1930) as Senta in *Der fliegende Holländer*. Photo Radio Times Hulton Picture Library.

Cornelius Bronsgeest (1878–1957) in *Der fliegende Holländer*. Photo Radio Times Hulton Picture Library.

42 First page of the prose sketch for *Tannhäuser*. Richard Wagner Archiv, Bayreuth.

43 Joseph Tichatschek as Tannhäuser. Engraving, nineteenth century. Festspiele Bildarchiv, Bayreuth.

Johanna Wagner (1826–94), Wagner's niece, as Elisabeth in the first performance of *Tannhäuser*, Dresden 1845. Daguerreotype. Photo Radio Times Hulton Picture Library.

44 Act II, Scene 2 of the première of *Tannhäuser*, Dresden, 19 October 1845. After a watercolour by Wilhelm Heine.

44–45 Costumes for Tannhäuser, Elisabeth, the Landgrave and Wolfram. Copies of designs by Flinzer for the *Tannhäuser* première at Dresden, 1845. Theatermuseum, Munich.

47 Franz Liszt (1811–86). Portrait in oils by Miklós Barabás, 1847. Magyar Nemzeti Muzeum, Budapest.

Poster announcing the première of *Lohengrin* at Weimar, 28 August 1850. Richard Wagner Gedenkstätte der Stadt Bayreuth.

Stage designs by Wagner for the Weimar première of *Lohengrin*. Nationalarchiv der Richard-Wagner-Stiftung, Bayreuth.

49 *Prelude to Lohengrin*. Oil painting by Henri Fantin-Latour, 1902. Musée du Petit-Palais, Paris. Photo Bulloz.

50 Design for the costume of Lohengrin by Julius Schnorr von Carolsfeld, 1860. Photo Radio Times Hulton Picture Library.

Title page of the libretto of *Lohengrin*, Weimar, 1850. Richard Wagner Archiv, Bayreuth.

51 The old opera-house and the Zwingerstrasse burning in the May uprising, Dresden, 1849. Lithograph. Photo Deutsche Fotothek Dresden.

52 Warrant of arrest for Wagner issued by the City Police Commission, Dresden, 16 May 1849. Photo Radio Times Hulton Picture Library.

53 Title page of the first impression of Wagner's 'Die Kunst und die Revolution', Leipzig, 1849.

56 Mathilde Wesendonk (1828–1902) and her son Guido. Pastel by E.B. Kietz, Paris, December 1856. Richard Wagner Museum, Triebschen.

Richard Wagner. Photograph, 1859. Photo Radio Times Hulton Picture Library.

57 View of Zürich, with the Wesendonk villa on the left. Watercolour, 1857. Frau Heck-Rieter, Zürich.

Wagner's 'Asyl'. Pencil drawing, c. 1857. Frau Heck-Rieter, Zürich.

58 Otto Wesendonk (1815–96). Photograph, c. 1860. Dr Jurg Wille, Meilen, Switzerland.

59 The last page of the compositional sketch for *Das Rheingold*, completed 14 January 1854. Richard Wagner Archiv, Bayreuth.

60 Minna Wagner (1809–66). Watercolour by Clementine Stockar-Escher, Zürich, 1853. Richard Wagner Gedenkstätte der Stadt Bayreuth.

61 Title page of the parody of *Tannhäuser* by Carl Binders (1816–60), 1857. Stadtbibliothek, Vienna.

Title page of the first edition of Baudelaire's (1821–67) 'Richard Wagner et Tannhauser à Paris', Paris, 1861. Richard Wagner Gedenkstätte der Stadt Bayreuth.

62 Design by Philippe Chaperon for Act II, Scene 3 of the Paris production of *Tannhäuser*, 1861. Bibliothèque Nationale, Paris.

64 *Tannhäuser and Venus* by Eugène Delacroix (1798–1863). Gouache. Werner Coninx-Stiftung, Zürich.

66 *Tannhäuser on the Venusberg* by Joseph Aigner. Mural, 1881. Schloss Neuschwanstein. Photo Werner Neumeister.

Tannhäuser – the Song Contest by Joseph Aigner. Mural, 1881. Schloss Neuschwanstein. Photo Werner Neumeister.

67 Cosima (1837–1930) with her father Franz Liszt. Photograph. Nationalarchiv der Richard-Wagner-Stiftung, Bayreuth.

Hans von Bülow (1830–94). Photograph. Nationalarchiv der Richard-Wagner-Stiftung, Bayreuth.

68 King Ludwig II of Bavaria (1845–86). Portrait by F. Dürck, 1864. Richard Wagner Gedenkstätte der Stadt Bayreuth.

Schloss Berg on Lake Starnberg.

Coloured lithograph. Staatliche Graphische Sammlungen, Munich.

69 Wagner escorts Cosima through the streets of Munich after a rehearsal of *Tristan und Isolde* in 1865, while Hans von Bülow follows with the music. Cartoon by M. Schultze. Private collection.

70 Arthur Schopenhauer (1788–1860). Photo Radio Times Hulton Picture Library.

The Residenz (Royal Palace) and the Court Theatre, Munich. Lithograph. Stadtmuseum, Munich.

71 Playbill for the première of *Tristan und Isolde* in Munich on 10 June 1865. Theatermuseum, Munich.

Ludwig and Malvina Schnorr von Carolsfeld as Tristan and Isolde, Munich, 1865. Photograph. Theatermuseum, Munich.

72 Costumes for Tristan and Isolde for the Munich première of *Tristan und Isolde*, 1865. Designs by Franz Seitz. Bayerische Staatliche Schlösser, Gärten und Seen, Munich.

Costumes for Melot and Brangaene for the 1865 Munich première of *Tristan und Isolde*. Designs by Franz Seitz. Theatermuseum, Munich.

73 Stage design by Angelo Quaglio II for Act III in the Munich première of *Tristan und Isolde*, 1865. Wittelsbacher Ausgleichsfond, Munich.

74 Pencil drawing of Wagner by Auguste Renoir (1841–1919) after the photograph by L. Pierson, Paris, October–November 1867. Musée Marmottan, Paris.

Cosima Liszt (1837–1930). Detail of a drawing by Friedrich Preller, Weimar, 1855. Richard Wagner Archiv, Bayreuth.

75 *Tristan und Isolde, Act II: The Signal in the Night.* Pencil drawing by Henri Fantin-Latour, *c.* 1885. Musée du Petit-Palais, Paris. Photo Bulloz.

76 Triebschen by Lake Lucerne. Copy of a lost watercolour. Richard Wagner Gedenkstätte der Stadt Bayreuth.

77 King Ludwig II of Bavaria (1845–86). Painting by Carl von Piloty, 1865. Bayerische Staatsgemäldesammlungen, Munich.

78 Act I, Scene 1 of *Die Meistersinger von Nürnberg*. Drawing by Theodor Pixis, Munich, 1868. Wittelsbacher Ausgleichsfond, Munich.

79 'Wach' auf' chorus of *Die Meistersinger*. *Illustrirte Zeitung*, Leipzig, 1 August 1868.

80 Act III, Scene 5 of *Die Meistersinger*. Stage design by Heinrich Döll, Munich, 1868. Wittelsbacher Ausgleichsfond, Munich.

Costumes for Eva and Stolzing for the première of *Die Meistersinger* in Munich, 1868. Designs by Franz Seitz. Richard Wagner Gedenkstätte der Stadt Bayreuth.

81 *Die Meistersinger von Nürnberg*. Oil painting by Eduard Ille, 1866. Wittelsbacher Ausgleichsfond, Munich.

83 Cosima Wagner (1837–1930). Photo Radio Times Hulton Picture Library.

Richard Wagner (1813–83). Photo Radio Times Hulton Picture Library.

84 Caricature of Wagner by Gill. Cover of *L'Eclipse*, Paris, 18 April 1869.

85 The Hofoper (Opera-House), Vienna. Steel engraving by C. Rorich after a drawing by L. Roh-

bock, *c.* 1870. Historisches Museum der Stadt Wien, Vienna.

Eduard Hanslick (1825–1904). Photograph by Fritz Luckhardt, *c.* 1880. Historisches Museum der Stadt Wien, Vienna.

86 Friedrich Nietzsche (1844–1900). Photograph. Nationalarchiv der Richard-Wagner-Stiftung, Bayreuth.

Title page of the first edition of Nietzsche's *Die Geburt der Tragödie aus dem Geiste der Musik*, Leipzig, 1872.

87 Wagner at Triebschen. Photograph, 1868. Photo Radio Times Hulton Picture Library.

88 *Das Rheingold*. Engraving after Theodor Pixis' drawing. *Illustrirte Zeitung*, Leipzig, 23 October 1869.

89 Playbill for the première of *Das Rheingold*, Munich, 22 September 1869. Theatermuseum, Munich.

90 Support machinery for the Rhinemaidens behind the scenes of the 1876 production of *Das Rheingold*, Bayreuth. Contemporary engraving. Photo Festspiele Bildarchiv, Bayreuth.

91 The closing scene of *Das Rheingold*. Drawing by Theodor Pixis, Munich, 1869.

Franz Betz (1835–1900) as Wotan at Bayreuth, 1876. Photograph. Nationalarchiv der Richard-Wagner-Stiftung, Bayreuth.

Hans Hotter (b. 1908) as Wotan at Bayreuth, 1956. Photograph. Nationalarchiv der Richard-Wagner-Stiftung, Bayreuth.

92 Act II, Scene 4 and Act III, Scene 2 of *Die Walküre*. Drawings by Theodor Pixis, 1870. Wittelsbacher Ausgleichsfond, Munich.

93 Amalie Materna (1844–1918). Photo Radio Times Hulton Picture Library.

Joseph Nierung as Hunding at Bayreuth, 1876. Photograph. Richard Wagner Archiv, Bayreuth.

Kirsten Flagstad (1895–1962) as Brünnhilde in *Die Walküre*. Photograph. Royal Opera House Archives, London.

94 Richard and Cosima Wagner. Photograph by Fritz Luckhardt, Vienna, 1872. Richard Wagner Gedenkstätte der Stadt Bayreuth.

95 Otto von Bismarck (1815–98) as 'unified Germany' with Europe under his control. Cartoon from *Kladderadatsch*, Berlin, 1875.

The Opernring (Ring), Vienna. Coloured lithograph by Franz Alt, 1872. Historisches Museum der Stadt Wien, Vienna.

97 Cartoons of Wagner's concert in Vienna, 1 March 1875. Front page of the Viennese humorous weekly *Kikeriki*, 4 March 1875.

98 Exterior of the Festival Theatre, Bayreuth. Photograph, 1876. Richard Wagner Archiv, Bayreuth.

Interior of the Festival Theatre, Bayreuth. Drawing, 1875–6. Photo Festspiele Bildarchiv, Bayreuth.

99 Exterior of Wahnfried, Bayreuth. Photograph. Richard Wagner Archiv, Bayreuth.

Wilhelmine Schröder-Devrient as Classical Tragedy, Ludwig Schnorr von Carolsfeld as Germanic Myth and Cosima Wagner as Music with her son Siegfried by her side. Sgraffito by Robert Krausse above the entrance of Wahnfried. Richard Wagner Archiv, Bayreuth.

100–101 *Der Ring des Nibelungen*: engravings after drawings by Knut Ekwall after the first performances at Bayreuth. *Das Rheingold*, first scene; *Die Walküre*, Act II, Scene 5; *Siegfried*, Act III, Scene 3; *Götterdämmerung*, Act III, Scene 2. *Illustrirte Zeitung*, Leipzig, 16 and 30 September 1876.

103 Winifred Wagner (b. 1897) seated at a table with the conductors Wilhelm Furtwängler (1886–1958) and Arturo Toscanini (1867–1957) during the 1931 Bayreuth Festival. Photo Bilderdienst Süddeutscher Verlag, Munich.

Winifred Wagner welcoming Adolf Hitler to the Bayreuth Festival, 1939. Photo Bilderdienst Süddeutscher Verlag, Munich.

104 George Bernard Shaw (1856–1950). Photograph by Elliott & Fry, 1891. Photo Elliott & Fry Bassano Ltd, London.

105 Georg Unger (1837–87) as Siegfried in *Götterdämmerung* at Bayreuth, 1876. Photograph. Nationalarchiv der Richard-Wagner-Stiftung, Bayreuth.

Ernst Kraus (1863–1941) and Hans Breuer (1868–1929) in *Siegfried*. Photo Radio Times Hulton Picture Library.

Lauritz Melchior (1890–1973) as Siegfried, *c.* 1928. Photo Radio Times Hulton Picture Library.

Paul Richter as Siegfried in the silent film *Siegfrieds Tod*, 1923, directed by Fritz Lang. Film still. Photo courtesy of National Film Archive, London.

106 Eva (1867–1942), Siegfried (1869–1930), Isolde (1865–1919), Daniela (1860–1940) as Senta and Blandine (1862–1941) as Elisabeth in costume for Wagnerian roles. Photograph. Richard Wagner Gedenkstätte der Stadt Bayreuth.

Siegfried as young Siegfried in the original costume for the 1876 production of *Siegfried* and Isolde as Isolde in the costume for the 1886 production of *Tristan und Isolde*. Photographs. Richard Wagner Gedenkstätte der Stadt Bayreuth.

107 Cosima and Richard Wagner with their son Siegfried. Photograph. Richard Wagner Gedenkstätte der Stadt Bayreuth.

108 Section of the Bayreuth Festival Theatre, from *Das Bühnenfestspielhaus zu Bayreuth*, Leipzig, 1873.

The orchestra at the Bayreuth Festival during a rehearsal, 1882. Coloured drawing by a member of the orchestra. Richard Wagner Gedenkstätte der Stadt Bayreuth.

109 Judith Gautier-Mendès (1846–1917). Photograph by Nadar, Paris, 1875. Richard Wagner Archiv, Bayreuth.

110 Paul von Joukowsky, Hermann Levi and Karl Brandt. Photograph, Bayreuth, 1882. Nationalarchiv der Richard-Wagner-Stiftung, Bayreuth.

111 Costume for Kundry in Act II and stage set for the closing scene of Act III of *Parsifal*. Designs by Paul von Joukowsky for the 1882 performance at Bayreuth. Richard Wagner Gedenkstätte der Stadt Bayreuth.

113 Emil Scaria as Gurnemanz, Amalie Materna as Kundry and Hermann Winkelmann as Parsifal in the 1882 production of *Parsifal* at Bayreuth. Photograph by Hans Brand. Bayerische Staatsbibliothek, Munich.

Marianne Brandt as Kundry in *Parsifal*, Act II, at Bayreuth, 1882. Photograph by Hans Brand. Bayerische Staatsbibliothek, Munich.

Klingsor's magic garden in *Parsifal*,

125

Act II. Oil painting by Max Brückner based on Paul von Joukowsky's set design for the Bayreuth première. Richard Wagner Gedenkstätte der Stadt Bayreuth.

114 Wieland Wagner (1917–66), Adolf Hitler and Wolfgang Wagner (b. 1919) photographed at Bayreuth, c. 1935. Photo Bilderdienst Süddeutscher Verlag, Munich.

115 Temple of the Holy Grail from a production of *Parsifal* at Bayreuth in the 1930s. Set designed by Wieland Wagner. Photograph. Festspiele Bildarchiv, Bayreuth.

The Temple of the Holy Grail. Oil painting by Max Brückner based on Paul von Joukowsky's set design for *Parsifal*. Richard Wagner Gedenkstätte der Stadt Bayreuth.

116 Palazzo Vendramin-Calergi, Venice, from the canal side. Coloured engraving. Biblioteca Nazionale Marciana, Venice.

117 Drawing of Wagner by Paul von Joukowsky, inscribed by Cosima 'R. reading, 12 Febr. 1883'. Richard Wagner Gedenkstätte der Stadt Bayreuth.

118 Wagner's grave in the garden of Wahnfried, photographed immediately after the funeral. Photo Radio Times Hulton Picture Library.

119 *Siegfried, Act III: Evocation of Erda.* Pencil sketch by Henri Fantin-Latour, c. 1885. Musée du Petit-Palais, Paris. Photo Bulloz.

INDEX

Page numbers in italics indicate illustrations

ALBERT, Alfred 65
Apel, Theodor 16, 25
'Art and Revolution' 53, 53–4
'Art-Work of the Future, The' 53–4
Austro-Prussian War 78

BAKUNIN, Mikhail 51
Ban on Love, The, see Liebesverbot, Das
Baudelaire, Charles 61, 118
Bayreuth Festival Theatre 37, 81, 90, 91, 98, 102, 108; finance for 95–7, 109; Nazism at 81, 104
Beardsley, Aubrey 118
Beethoven, Ludwig van 10, 17, 27–9
Bellini, Vincenzo 12, 15, 15–16, 18

Berger, Rudolf 33
Berlin, opera-house in 29, 37; revolution in 51
Berlioz, Hector 24, 25, 26
Betz, Franz 91
Beyond Good and Evil (Nietzsche) 86
Binders, Carl 61
Birth of Tragedy from the Spirit of Music, The (Nietzsche) 86, 87
Bismarck, Otto von 95
Brahms, Johannes 90
Brandt, Karl 110
Breuer, Hans 105
Brockhaus, Hermann 20
Brockhaus, Ottilie (Wagner's sister) 20

Bronsgeest, Cornelius 41
Brückner, Max 113, 115
Bülow, Hans von 63, 65, 67, 69, 69, 77–8, 83, 89
Bulwer-Lytton, Henry 20

Capuleti ed i Montecchi, I (Bellini) 15, 16
Cézanne, Paul 118
Chaperon, Philippe 62
Columbus Overture 24
'Communication to my Friends, A' 35, 48

DEBUSSY, Claude 116
Delacroix, Eugène 64

Destinn, Emmy *41*
Dettmer, Paul *31*
Döll, Heinrich *80, 89*
Don Giovanni (Mozart) 10, 16
Dresden Court Theatre 26, 30, *32*, 37, 40, 43, *51*

EKWALL, K. *100, 101*
'Ende in Paris, Ein' (An End in Paris) 27
Evocation of Erda (Fantin-Latour) *119*

FANTIN-LATOUR, Henri *49*, 75, 118, *119*
Feen, Die (The Fairies) 12, *13*, 14–16, 34; *leitmotifs* in 50; themes in 46
'Feminine Element in Humanity, The' 116
Fidelio (Beethoven) 10, 64
Flagstad, Kirsten *93*
fliegende Holländer, Der (The Flying Dutchman) 22, 24, 27, 29, 35, 37, *38, 39*, 41, 43, 48, *102*; productions of 30, 37, 40; themes in 35–6, 46
Franck, César 118
Franco-Prussian War 95
Franz Josef, Emperor 85
Freischütz, Der (Weber) 8
Furtwängler, Wilhelm *103*

GAUTIER, Théophile 109, 118
Gautier-Mendès, Judith *109*, 109
'German Art and German Politics' 84
Gesamtkunstwerk 54, 101
Geyer, Johanna (Wagner's mother) 6, 6–8, 29, *51*
Geyer, Karl Friedrich 8
Geyer, Ludwig (Wagner's stepfather) 6, 6–8
Gluck, Felix 54
Götterdämmerung 52, 75, 83, *101*; *see also Ring des Nibelungen, Der*
'glücklicher Abend, Ein' (A Happy Evening) 27
Guntram (R. Strauss) 118
Gutman, Robert W. 112

HABENECK, François 24
Handel, George Frederick 54
Hanslick, Eduard 74, *85*, 85
Heine, Heinrich 24, 35, 36, 37, 40
'Heldentum und Christentum' (Heroism and Christianity) 112
Hitler, Adolf 81, 102, *103*, 114, *114*
Hochzeit, Die (The Wedding) 12
Hoffman, E.T.A. 9

homosexuality 69, 87, 112
Hotter, Hans *91*
Humperdinck, Engelbert 116

IBSEN, Heinrich 36
Ille, Eduard *81*

JAHN, Friedrich Ludwig 84
Jank, Christian *89*
'Jewishness in Music' 53, 54–5, 85
Jews in Wagner's life and works 18, 20, 23, 24, 27, 55–6, 81, 110–14; Wandering Jew 35–7
Joachim, Joseph 90
Jockey Club of Paris 60–4
Joukowsky, Paul von *110, 111, 113, 115, 117*
Jullien, Adolphe 75

KAINZ, Josef 112
Kaisermarsch 95
Kotzebue, A.F.F. von 84
Kraus, Ernst *105*
Krausse, Robert *99*
Kriete, Henriette *21*

LANG, Fritz *105*
Lanner, Joseph 12
Leipzig 9, 12, 15, 16; St Thomas's Church and School 7; Wagner residence 5
leitmotif 50, 100
Leubald und Adelaide 9–10
Levi, Hermann 55, *110*, 110–12
Liebesverbot, Das (The Ban on Love) 18–19, *19*, 24, 34
Liszt, Franz 46, 47, 52, 58, 67, 90, 102
Logier, Johann Bernhard 10; *Method of Thorough-Bass* 10
Lohengrin 47, 49, 50, 102; composition of 45, 46; production of 52; themes in 48–50
London, Wagner festival in 109
Lucerne, Lake 76, *76*
Ludwig I of Bavaria 69–70
Ludwig II of Bavaria 68, 77; patron of Wagner 67–70, 75–8, 82, 84, 89–90; finances Bayreuth 96–7; opposes Wagner 110–12

MAGDEBURG, opera company of 16, 18
Mallarmé, Stéphane 118
Marschner, Heinrich August 12, 15–16, 18
Materna, Amalie *93*

Mein Leben 9, 25, 45, 52, 63, 89
Meistersinger von Nürnberg, Die 46, 65, 76, 78, *78*, 79, *79*, 80, 112; politics of 78–82, 84–5
Meistersinger von Nürnberg, Die (Ille) *81*
Melchior, Lauritz *105*
Memoirs of Herr von Schnabelewopski (Heine) 35
Mendelssohn-Bartholdy, Felix *14*, *15*, 55
Mendès, Catulle 109
Metternich, Princess 60, 64
Meyerbeer, Giacomo 12, 23, 24–5, 29, *31*, 55
Möller, Abraham 20
Montez, Lola 70
Morelli (baritone) 62, 63
Mottl, Felix 58
Mozart, Wolfgang Amadeus 10, 54, 118
Munich, Court Theatre and Royal Palace of 70; Wagner in 69–70, 75, 90

NAZISM, Wagner and 6, 81, 84, 102
Nerval, Gérard de 118
Neuschwanstein Castle 66
Niemann, Albert 62
Nierung, Joseph *93*
Nietzsche, Friedrich 86, *86*–7, 96, 104, *114*
Norma (Bellini) 15

OFFENBACH, Jacques 95
'Opera and Drama' 53

PARIS, revolution in 51; Wagner in 24, 26–7, 52, 59–64
Paris Opéra 24, *25*, 59–64, *62*
Parsifal 12, 18, 55–6, *111, 113, 115*; themes in 36, 40, 109–14
Pelléas et Mélisande (Debussy) 116
Perfall, Baron von 90
Perfect Wagnerite, The (Shaw) 104
'Pilgerfahrt zu Beethoven, Eine' (A Pilgrimage to Beethoven) 27
Planer, Amalie 20
Planer, Minna, *see* Wagner, Minna
Porges, Tausig and Heinrich 55
Prelude to Lohengrin (Fantin-Latour) *49*

QUAGLIO, Angelo *73*, *89*

RAIMUND, magic plays of 12
Redon, Odilon 118
Reinhold, Herr *38*
'Religion and Art' 112
Renoir, Jean 74, 118
'Revolution, The' 51

Reyer, Ernest (pseud.) 116
Rheingold, Das 56–8, 59, 83, 88, 89, 89, *90*, 90, *91*, 100, 102; *see also Ring des Nibelungen, Der*
Richard Wagner (Jullien) 75
'Richard Wagner and *Tannhäuser* in Paris' (Baudelaire) 61
Richter, Hans 89–90, 102
Richter, Paul *105*
Rienzi (Bulwer-Lytton) 20
Rienzi 21, 23, *30–1*, 33, 34; staged 26, 30–1, 33–4; *leitmotifs* in 50
Ring des Nibelungen, Der 54, 83, *91*, *92*, *93*, 100, *101*, 105; themes in 100–1, 104; *leitmotifs* in 50, 100–1; librettos of 56, 78; productions of 89–90, 95–7, 102; criticism of 102–4; *see also Rheingold, Das*; *Walküre, Die*; *Siegfried*; *Götterdämmerung*
Robert le Diable (Meyerbeer) 12
Rohde, Erwin 86
Röhm, Ernst 112
Rubinstein, Josef 55

Saint-Saëns, Camille 90, 118
Sand, Karl 84
Sax, Marie 62
Schlesinger, Moritz 25
Schloss Berg 68
Schnorr von Carolsfeld, Julius *50*
Schnorr von Carolsfeld, Ludwig 71, *75*
Schnorr von Carolsfeld, Malvina 70, *71*
Schopenhauer, Arthur 48, *70*, 71, 87
Schröder-Devrient, Wilhelmine 10, *11*, 15, *16–17*, *30*, 30, *33*, *38*, 40, 43
Schumann, Robert 45
Scribe, Augustin 24
Seitz, Franz *72*, *80*
Semper, Gottfried 69; Court Theatre, Dresden *32*
Shakespeare, William 16, 18
Shaw, George Bernard *104*, 104
Siegfried 56, 83, *101*, *119*; *see also Ring des Nibelungen, Der*
Siegfried Idyll 83
Siegfrieds Tod (Lang) 105
Signal in the Night, The (Fantin-Latour) *75*
Strassburg, Gottfried von 71
Strauss, Johann 12
Strauss, Richard 118
Symbolists 118

Tannhäuser 18, *42*, 43, 44–5, 61, 62, 65, 66; ballet in 60–4; productions of 43,
52, 59–64; themes in 46, 48, 73
Tannhäuser and Venus (Delacroix) *64*
'Tannhäuser Quadrille und Walzer' (Binders) *61*
Tchaikovsky, Peter Illyich 102
Tedesco, Fortunata 62, *63*
Thus Spake Zarathustra (Nietzsche) 86
Tichatschek, Joseph 21, *30*, 30, *43*, 43
Toscanini, Arturo *103*
'To the German Army Before Paris' 95
Triebschen, Villa 76, *76*, 83–4, 86, 90
Tristan und Isolde half-title, 54, 69, 71, *72*, *73*, 75, 83, 102, 112; composition of 56, 58, 71; production of 70; themes in 46, 71–4, 78, 79, 87
Trojans, The (Berlioz) 26
Tyszkiewicz, Count Vincnz 12

Unger, Georg *105*

Vampyr, Der (Marschner) 12, 15
Vendramin, Palazzo 116, *116*
Venice, Wagner in 58, 64, 116
Verdi, Giuseppe 5–6, 14, 118
Vienna, revolution in 51; Wagner visits 12, 64; Opera-House *85*, *96*

Wächter, Michael *31*, *38*, 40
Wagner, Adolph (Wagner's uncle) 10, *10*
Wagner, Cäcilie (Wagner's sister, later married to Eduard Avenarius) 24
Wagner, Cosima (*née* Liszt, first married to von Bülow) 65, 67, 69, *69*, 70, 74, 75–8, 82–3, *83*, 89, *94*, *107*, 109
Wagner, Eva (Wagner's daughter) 78, *106*
Wagner, Isolde (Wagner's daughter) *106*
Wagner, Johanna, *see* Geyer, Johanna
Wagner, Johanna (Wagner's niece) *43*, 43
Wagner, Julius (Wagner's brother) 8
Wagner, Karl Friedrich 6
Wagner, Luisa (Wagner's sister) 9
Wagner, Minna (*née* Planer, Wagner's first wife) 16, 17, 18, 19–22, 24, 29, 37, 51–2, 59, 60, 65, 70, 109
Wagner, Ottilie, *see* Brockhaus, Ottilie
Wagner, Richard: politics 5–6, 46, 51–2, 81, 104; family 6–8, 9; education 7–10, 11–12; employment 12, 16, 43; anti-Semitism 16, 23–4, 54–6, 85–7, 104, 110–14; first marriage 19–21, 23–5, 51–2, 65, 70; debts 17, 20–1, 24, 29–30, 51, 70, 96, 109;
travels 21–2, 24–7, 59–65, 109; lack of humour 37; character 52–5; mistresses 56–8, 109, 112; and Ludwig II 67–70, 75–8, 82, 89, 96–7, 109–12; nationalism 81; second marriage 83; view of Christianity 112–14; death 116; influence 116–18; musical career: early compositions 11–15; first opera 12, 14–16; C major symphony 12; influences on work 15–16, 18, 31, 71–3; themes of works 35–6, 40, 46–8, 100–1, 104, 110–14; romantic work 46; music-drama 46, 48, 73–5, 78–9, 112; *see also* titles of works; literary career: early writing 9–10; autobiography 9, 25, 45, 52, 63, 89; short stories 27–9; notes on *The Flying Dutchman* 35–6, 40; political essays 51–5, 84–7, 112; librettos 54, 73–5, 82, 112; poetry and drama 95; *see also* titles of works; illustrations of: portraits and cartoons *frontispiece*, *16*, *28*, *36*, *56*, *69*, *74*, *83*, *84*, *87*, *94*, *97*, *107*, *117*; warrant for arrest *52*; house in Zürich *57*; grave of *118*
Wagner, Rosalie (Wagner's sister) 9, *9*
Wagner, Siegfried (Wagner's son) 55, *106*, *107*
Wagner, Wieland *114*, *115*
Wagner, Winifred (Wagner's daughter-in-law) *103*
Wagner, Wolfgang *114*
Wahnfried, Villa *99*, 109, *118*
Walküre, Die 56, 58, 83, *92*, *93*; performance of 90; *see also Ring des Nibelungen, Der*
Weber, Carl Maria von *8*, 8, 15, 18
Wedding, The, see Hochzeit, Die
Weimar, Wagner in 52, 64
Weinlig, Christian Theodor 12
Wesendonk, Guido *56*
Wesendonk Lieder 58
Wesendonk, Mathilde 56, *56–8*, 71
Wesendonk, Otto 56, *58*, 58
Whistler, James McNeill 118
Will to Power, The (Nietzsche) 86
World as Will and Idea, The (Schopenhauer) 71
Wüllner, Franz 90
Würzburg, Wagner in 12, 15
Wüst, Henriette *30*

Zauberflöte, Die (The Magic Flute) (Mozart) 12
Zürich 57; Wagner in 52, 56, 58